## Testimonies for *Throwing Grapes and Moving Mountains*

I have read dozens of devotional books over the years, but never before have I found one as steeped in Scripture as Jan's. Her Spirit-led writings have nurtured my soul in various ways. I have found comfort in my pain, hope in my despair, understanding in my isolation, consolation in my disappointment, correction in my complacency, grace in my lack, joy in my trials, and revelation in my confusion—leading me into a higher level of worship. These songs and devotionals have helped to nourish and restore me inwardly, for they are based on the Word of God; they offer the daily bread and water of life that we human beings desperately need and will thrive on. The Lord has used them to stir a spiritual hunger and thirst, spurring me on to a deeper commitment to Christ by adding substance to my good intentions of obedience to Him. So don't just browse over the rich truths presented here; embrace these whispers from God, apply them to your life, and find the unspeakable joy of knowing Jesus progressively better!

Mary Koster
Teaching Director,
Community Bible Study

For me, receiving a devotion from Jan is like a kiss on the cheek from my heavenly Father. I look forward to the prayer time I will have meditating on the words God has breathed into her and she obediently shares. It is like entering a warm cabin from the cold, arctic snow and having the most delicious, nutritious, meaty stew waiting to fill me and comfort me. Jan's devotions are like the stew; they are meaty and full of God's words of love and encouragement. They challenge me to go deeper with Him and recognize the strong and fierce love that God, my Father, has for me. Thank you, Jan.

Cindy Purdy

Jan's devotions have the unique ability to draw you into the very presence of God. What a gift it is to hear Him speak directly to you individually so that you can internalize and apply to your life that day's life lesson. I thank God for Jan's ability to hear and share what God speaks to her with others in such a powerful way. She truly is a pen in God's hand as she allows Him to work through her to bless others.

Paula Felsing
Area Director,
Community Bible Study

# Throwing Grapes and Moving Mountains

# Throwing Grapes and Moving Mountains

A Devotional Journey for the Hungry Heart

Jan Hegelein

WESTBOW

PRESS

A DIVISION OF THOMAS NELSON

WestBow Press books may be ordered through booksellers or by contacting:

WestBow Press
A Division of Thomas Nelson
1663 Liberty Drive
Bloomington, IN 47403
www.westbowpress.com
1-(866) 928-1240

Scripture taken from the NEW AMERICAN STANDARD BIBLE®, Copyright © 1960,1962,1963,1968,1971,1972,1973,1975,1977,19 95 by The Lockman Foundation. Used by permission.

Scripture taken from the Holy Bible, New International Version®. Copyright © 1973, 1978, 1984 Biblica. Used by permission of Zondervan. All rights reserved.

ISBN: 978-1-4497-7590-2 (sc)
ISBN: 978-1-4497-7592-6 (e)
ISBN: 978-1-4497-7593-3 (hc)

Library of Congress Control Number: 2012921482

Printed in the United States of America

WestBow Press rev. date: 11/30/2012

For Bruce Hegelein
My strongest encourager, best friend, and wonderful husband

# Contents

# Preface

As I have written these devotions, it has been my heart's cry to know a fuller measure of God's grace and witness the incomparable manifestation of His glory fall down upon this earth. How I long to see a fresh wind of God blow throughout this land, drawing each and every person first to repentance and then to a lifestyle of abandoned worship of our King. Is this too much to ask? Not if we serve an almighty God! He *loves* to bless His children so we may be a blessing to all those around us. Will we choose to walk in humble submission and glorious obedience to the King of all kings and the Savior of our souls? Or will we continue to lean on our own understanding and walk according to the principalities of this world?

By the grace of God and the leading of the Holy Spirit, let us join together and ask God to examine our hearts, redirect our steps, and so fill us with Himself that the aroma of Jesus surrounds us wherever we go, and the glory of the Lord will once again begin to pour out over this land!

Let's put on our spiritual running shoes and lunge into the mighty arms of an almighty God!

> Lord, fill us with *grapes of blessing* so huge that they will feed our neighbors. Give us gleanings from the Word of God so rich, full, and deep that their substance will be like sweet grape juice flowing down into our hearts.

By God's grace, let us pick up those huge grapes and share their fruit so the blessings of God will flow like divine wine into others' hearts. In the process, may our prayers be energized to move *the mountains of unbelief and doubt* that so often hinder a vibrant life in Christ.

I pray this sampling of devotions will encourage you, challenge you, and cause you to fall even more deeply in love with the Lover of your soul!

As they were passing by in the morning, they saw the fig tree withered from the roots up. Being reminded, Peter said to Him, "Rabbi, look, the fig tree which You cursed has withered." And Jesus answered saying to them, "Have faith in God. Truly I say to you, whoever says to this mountain, 'Be taken up and cast into the sea,' and does not doubt in his heart, but believes that what he says is going to happen, it will be granted him. Therefore I say to you, all things for which you pray and ask, believe that you have received them, and they will be granted you. Whenever you stand praying, forgive, if you have anything against anyone, so that your Father who is in heaven will also forgive you your transgressions. (Mark 11:20–25)

How is the land, is it fat or lean? Are there trees in it or not? Make an effort then to get some of the fruit of the land." Now the time was the time of the first ripe grapes. So they went up and spied out the land from the wilderness of Zin as far as Rehob, at Lebo-hamath. When they had gone up into the Negev, they came to Hebron where Ahiman, Sheshai and Talmai, the descendants of Anak were (Now Hebron was built seven years before Zoan in Egypt.) Then they came to the valley of Eshcol and from there cut down a branch with a single cluster of grapes; and they carried it on a pole between two men, with some of the pomegranates and the figs. That place was called the valley of Eshcol, because of the cluster which the sons of Israel cut down from there. (Num. 13:20–24)

# Laying It Down—an Intercessor's Prayer

Father, as I once again attempt to enter into the battle through prayer, will this time be any better than any other attempt? Not if I depend on myself. Help me, Lord, to once again draw aside to listen and seek Your heart. There is much that consumes my soul and many concerns that battle for my attention, yet You tell me to be at peace, for You will never abandon me. How great and awesome and mighty is the wonderful love of God!

Father, as I come to You, I lay my burdens before Your feet. Give me the grace, dear Lord, to leave them with You. May I pick up only those burdens You want me to offer back to You on this journey of intercession. I was not meant to be a burden-bearing creature. If I attempt to carry more into the prayer room than You have called me to cry out for, I will become too discouraged, too weary, and too worn out to be of any good to anyone. I need Your discernment, Daddy, to know what I am to labor in prayer over and what I am to leave at Your feet. I do not have the discernment, knowledge, wisdom, or power to lead me along this road of intercession. So I beg of You, dear Lord, to grant me discernment and trust—discernment to know where You are calling me to pray with fervency and trust to lay all other things at Your feet and leave them there.

This act of trust and laying things down at Your feet is in itself a beautiful act of worship, for it is here that I must come face to face with my Father who is holy, mighty, all powerful, faithful, righteous, and true. As I lay down the things my heart anguishes over and refuse to repetitively reclaim them, I am in essence proclaiming my God to be the almighty, all-knowing one. This is the essence of worship in its simplest and truest form. It is worship both on an emotional and a practical level. It says, "I trust My Father and will choose to wait for His deliverance and provision to see me through."

So today, as I seek Your direction, Lord, for my time of prayer, let me hear Your heart and pray over those things You have chosen for me today. It is in this work that I truly become a co-laborer with God, praying according to the dictates of the Father's heart. Fill my heart with Your passions to engage in the battle. May all the honor go to You, today and every day.

Amen.

> Rejoice always; pray without ceasing; in everything give thanks; for this is God's will for you in Christ Jesus. (1 Thess. 5:16–18)

# Acknowledgments

Several people have been integral in the process of writing of this book. My dear friends Mary, Cindy, Diane, Sue, Jodi, Brenda, Karen, and Paula, your prayers and encouragement throughout each step of this journey have been invaluable. Without your support, I may not have had the fortitude to see this project through to completion. Carol, your grace in editing has truly been a labor of love. Thank you, dear friend, for all your skill and support. Most of all, I give much thanks to my heavenly Father, who has inspired me, strengthened me, and given me the courage to share the insights He has provided.

# Introduction

This devotion book has been compiled from a collection of inspirational pieces written for a local Bible study. The original intent of the devotions was to encourage and equip the study's leaders in their ministry roles. They have been enthusiastically received, thus prompting my desire to see them shared on a wider level. This body of work represents several years of sitting at God's feet and listening to His voice through Scripture. I pray you will hear His heartbeat of love as you read through each selection.

The format is based on a weekly rotation. Five days are Scripture-based devotions. The weekends are a bit lighter, with Scripture-based lyrics and poems. My prayer is that you will find encouragement, hope, and a renewal of your love for Christ in the following pages. He is ever faithful!

—J. Hegelein

# 1

# Dance of the Redeemed

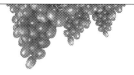

> He said, "I have been very zealous for the LORD, the God of hosts; for the sons of Israel have forsaken Your covenant, torn down Your altars and killed Your prophets with the sword and I alone am left; and they seek my life, to take it away." So He said, "Go forth and stand on the mountain before the LORD." And behold, the LORD was passing by! And a great and strong wind was rending the mountains and breaking in pieces the rocks before the LORD; but the LORD was not in the wind. And after the wind an earthquake, but the LORD was not in the earthquake. After the earthquake a fire, but the LORD was not in the fire; and after the fire a sound of a gentle blowing. When Elijah heard it, he wrapped his face in his mantle and went out and stood in the entrance of the cave and behold, a voice came to him and said, "What are you doing here, Elijah?"
> (1 Kings 19:10–12)

Prayer is a never-ending journey in the Christian life. It is the one discipline that can quickly discourage and repel us because we feel so inadequate in the way we practice and engage in its use. Yet at the same time, we heartily agree that it is the one spiritual tool that has the capacity to draw upon the resources of heaven and impact and change lives for the better. So why don't we pray more? Is more really the answer, or are the integrity and purity of a childlike dependence what we are really missing? We all acknowledge that we need prayer, and we quickly recognize those who have been well schooled in its discipline. If the deepest passion of any follower were to be unfolded and exposed, it would reveal a heart that secretly yearns for a deeper level of intimacy with its Creator. Yet the thing we desire the most is so often crowded out or completely ignored because to our common sensibilities, it seems too presumptuous and absolutely too preposterous to be considered. God. Creator. Redeemer. Holy One. Would He share His heart with one as lowly and insignificant as me?

The beginning of a God-birthed passion is often derailed by a false sense of humility or by fear of the unknown. False humility would proclaim that we are too insignificant for the Creator of the world to look down on and draw us into deeper levels of holiness. The more we listen to this lie, the more content we become in our present state of revelation. Eventually we become so complacent that we even lose the vision that there could be something deeper, more profound, sweeter, and more intensely holy than our present reality. We begin to sink back into the familiarity of what surrounds us. Our comfort levels rise once again, and we forget that there ever was a glimmer of hope that we might know Jesus in a more intimate, holy, and powerful way.

We begin to look around and measure ourselves against those who are also journeying on their faith walk. If we *only* measure ourselves against others' progress, we will totally miss out on the unique and exquisite journey God has planned for us as individuals. Fear can sneak in unawares and often gains a foothold in our spirits before we are even aware of its presence. It grows unnoticed at first until it cowers so large that it actually repels the seeker. The comfort monster again comes into play as we run toward that which is known and therefore "safe" rather than embracing what is new and uncertain because we cannot perceive the end product. Truly, if we could see the end, would it be a work of God or a creation of our own making? Fear is rooted in the lie that God cannot be trusted or depended upon. True faith declares, "I will trust in Him even though He slay me" (See Job 15:13). We still have far to go to walk in this type of faith!

The proverbial bush is blazing with God's holiness. The question is, will we take off our shoes and draw near? Or will we just watch the bush blaze from a distance and marvel at the courage of those who did take off their shoes? It is in this area of the pursuit of God's full measure of holiness and grace that contentment actually kills. It strikes a death blow to the passion and pursuit of the totality of God. There is always more of Him to be revealed, a deeper understanding of the power, purity, and passion of His love to be pursued. Yet we will never approach any of this unless we engage in the dance of the divine encounter.

This pursuit of God begins because He first seeks us. The intricacy of this dance is dependent on the sensitivity of our spirits to hear and heed the sweet, still voice of the Holy Spirit. This takes time, and it cannot be rushed. God will speak when He is ready. He will move on our hearts to pray, praise, and intercede with a purity and intensity we can now only imagine. He is waiting. He wants to pour His fullness into our spirits to fully equip us to run the race with endurance. Will we draw aside to listen? This is where effectual prayer is birthed—in the waiting room of the King. Stillness before God is completely cross cultural and the reason why so few enter into this exquisite divine dance. Will we draw aside to listen?

# 2

# Breathe on Me, Oh Spirit of God!

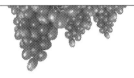

## The Cry of a Seeking Heart

> Now Moses was pasturing the flock of Jethro his father-in-law, the priest of Midian; and he led the flock to the west side of the wilderness and came to Horeb, the mountain of God. The angel of the LORD appeared to him in a blazing fire from the midst of a bush; and he looked, and behold, the bush was burning with fire, yet the bush was not consumed. So Moses said, "I must turn aside now and see this marvelous sight, why the bush is not burned up." When the LORD saw that he turned aside to look, God called to him from the midst of the bush and said, "Moses, Moses!" And he said, "Here I am." Then He said, "Do not come near here; remove your sandals from your feet, for the place on which you are standing is holy ground." (Ex. 3:1–5)

Let me be content in nothing but a full manifestation of God's glory upon this earth. If I am satisfied with what my eyes can see, I will never move into the fuller revelation of the glory of the Lord. Lord, let me dwell in the place of the burning bush where I *must* remove my shoes, my self-determination, and my own independence from You; *remove your shoes, for you are standing on holy ground.*

If I am walking in the Spirit, everywhere I walk is holy ground. Everything can be claimed as territory for the King. God is sending me out as the advance party to plant His flag in enemy territory through the prayer realm. Yes, He does tell me to be content in what I have, for He has promised that He will never leave me nor forsake me. But the critical question is, will I engage in the battle? He has provided for my every need. Therefore, I must proclaim the glories and majesty of the King wherever I am—in the neighborhood, the community stores, the schools, or the workplace. Wherever I travel, let me walk in that place and proclaim it as territory for the King of Kings—not by might or by strength but by the Spirit, says the Lord!

Arise, oh sleeper, awake from the dead!

Wake me up, Lord, that I may begin to walk in the full manifestation of Your power and glory. Breathe life into me, Jesus. May even my DNA be changed from mine to Yours! *I have nothing without You!* My ambitions aim too low, my prayers are too weak, my passions are too dull, and my expectations more often rest with what man can do rather than what God can do. You call me to lift my eyes unto the hills from whence Your help comes.

Teach me, Lord, to pray in a way that touches Your heart. Let my prayers line up with Your plans for this earth. Give wings to my prayers, my hope, my vision, and my passions. I need an extreme makeover. I am desperate for a fresh move of Your hand; I yearn to feel the drumbeat of heaven, the life force of heaven coursing through my veins. Lord, may it become my very blood! Oh Father, hover over me, and bear new life in me according to the Holy Spirit. Let me deny Him no longer!

Your thoughts are so much higher than my thoughts, oh Lord. You seek the soul and hearts of men. Let my heart, my being, my very essence be laid bare before the God with whom I have to do. You are the only reason I live and breathe. Let me live and breathe for You. Birth in me a jealous and zealous heart for Your glory to come down to earth. Let me hunger for nothing more than YOU! Remove from me futile and foolish thinking and expectations. Oh Lord, give me the grace to dream God-sized dreams, to walk in the full manifestation of who You are. Please, Father, part the mists just a little bit more so that, like Moses, I may catch just a glimpse of Your glory and be forever changed. Breathe life into me, oh God, a deep, pulsating Holy Spirit life. May I never again lean on my own understanding but walk in the fullness of who You are in me. Breath of heaven renew me, restore me, revive me, equip me, engage me, cleanse me, fortify me. Focus all of me, on *You*!

> Awake, awake, O Zion, clothe yourself with strength. Put on your garments of splendor, O Jerusalem, the holy city. The uncircumcised and defiled will not enter you again. Shake off your dust; rise up, sit enthroned, O Jerusalem. Free yourself from the chains on your neck, O captive Daughter of Zion. For this is what the LORD says: "You were sold for nothing, and without money you will be redeemed."
> (Isa. 52:1–3)

I am like that dead daughter of Israel. I need Jesus to fall down on me, to completely cover me and transform everything within me to line up with His life and nature and passion. Change me, oh Lord, and I shall be new. Restore me and I shall live. Fortify me that I may walk in the fullness of who You are! Glory be to God in the highest. Glory to God. Hallelujah. Amen.

# 3

# Enter His Gates

Even though I walk through the valley of the shadow of death,
I will fear no evil, for You are with me; Your rod and Your
staff, they comfort me. You prepare a table before me in the
presence of my enemies. You anoint my head with oil; my cup
overflows. Surely goodness and love will follow me all the days
of my life, and I will dwell in the house of the LORD forever.
(Ps. 23:4–6)

Wrestle with God; grab hold of those promises, and don't let go until they
are fulfilled. One of the enemy's most fruitful tactics is to wear down the
saints and cause them to give up in discouragement. Where have you lost
hope? Where have God-sized dreams ceased to tickle the imagination?
Where have you settled for just good enough? Do you believe you shall see
the salvation of your God—here and now? Line up with Jacob, and grab
hold of the Lord and declare, "I will not let go until You bless me" (Gen.
32:26). Even though you may limp as a result of this God encounter the
rest of your life, isn't it better to engage with God? He has so much in store
for you—heavenly treasures multiplied through your joyful obedience
combined with the power and strength of a pure heart gained through the
process of living an obedient life. As you trust in God and cling to Him
for all your needs and desires, you will discover an unadulterated vision of
your almighty God. With each dependent step, you will see Him a bit more
clearly and begin to hear and discern His voice more accurately. He calls
to you hunger after Him. With what are you satisfying your God-given
appetite? Nothing can completely fill your deepest longings—nothing but
more of God.

Will you pursue Him?

Will you bow before Him and confess you can't pursue Him without Him drawing you to do so?

It all comes back to the creative, powerful nature of our God. When will we, as the church, finally realize we can truly do nothing on our own? It is His hand that gives each breath; His hand that causes hearts to beat one more time; and His hand that holds us together so we don't just dissolve into dust this very moment. When this realization truly invades the heart, worship is offered with pure motives. It is His hand that encourages us to dream. It is His hand that holds us close in love. It is His hand that wipes every tear and comforts every broken heart—His hand.

When we stop taking credit for anything we do and cast all things as a thanksgiving offering before His feet, we begin to see and understand the parameters of this reality. God. The beginning and the end. Period. All that we are, all that we have, and all that we hope for is only because He, in His gracious love, has provided it. Let us prepare our hearts to offer a continual thanksgiving fest unto the only one who was, who is, and who reigns forever. Step aside from the battle for a moment to praise Him and give thanks. The righteous enter the gates of heaven with thanksgiving. Wouldn't it be good to start now? Do we want to see righteousness descend on this weary land? Let us give thanks!

> The LORD has chastened me severely, but He has not given me over to death. Open for me the gates of righteousness; I will enter and give thanks to the LORD. This is the gate of the LORD through which the righteous may enter.
> (Ps. 118:18–20)

# 4

# Double Portion

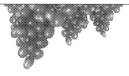

Instead of your shame you will have a double portion, and instead of humiliation they will shout for joy over their portion. Therefore they will possess a double portion in their land, everlasting joy will be theirs. (Isa. 61:7)

Wow! God gives such a blessing of joy—a *double* portion, a portion so abundant that the only response is to *shout*! How awesome are the gifts of God! He gives a double portion *in their land*. Do you believe that God wants to bless you right where you are now in your present circumstances? Can you trust Him to do that? Are you shouting for joy over the goodness of God?

It is God's nature to bless His children. He loves to pour out from the depths and riches of His heart to bless and guide. He does not want His kids to wear the cloak of shame or humiliation. Jesus came to break the bonds of sin, so why would anyone remain there? Man was not designed to be a bottom dweller but to ascend to the highest of heights with the wings of eagles and the Lord as the wind under His wings! Where are you lacking joy and a settled peace in your spirit? Do not remain there, beloved. Remember the lover of your soul, and turn to Him in all things for your sustenance, your strength, your joy, and your hope. He desires to bless you abundantly above all that you can ask or think. How great is our Father's love for you. How He desires to pour out into the soul whose heart is completely His. Will you receive all He has to give you?

The Lord's goodness will lead you into an everlasting joy, and nothing this world throws at you can thwart that joy if you will remain focused on God. At times this is a process, but know that as you trust in Him and push through the pain, joy is waiting at the other side! This joy is not only for you but is open to all who will come to Him with open hearts and hands. (Notice how the text moves from "you" to "they." God's love is extremely personal yet available to all!)

How can we, the forgiven ones, draw others in whom God desires to bless? By using the double portion He has blessed us with! It may be in the areas of our time, our talents or abilities, or even our finances. Never squander these gifts. Use them for the building up of the kingdom rather than hoarding them for personal pleasure. Hoarded blessings reveal the depth of the heart's passion to trust in those resources rather than looking unto God's daily provision for all needs. With this attitude, God's blessings will become like the manna in the wilderness, which grew moldy and rotten after one day. (See Ex. 16:15–21.) They become useless from an eternal perspective!

There is also another subtle trap the enemy uses to usurp the intent of God's blessing. It deals with the affections of the heart. Enjoy all the good things God has given as blessings, but be aware of the danger that lures the heart away to love the blessings rather than the one who blesses. Will we be like Job, who said, "The Lord gave and the Lord has taken away, blessed be the name of the Lord!" (Job 1:21–22), or will our possessions draw us away from the one we love, the one who redeemed us with His life's blood to the point that we worship the created things rather than the Creator? (See Matt. 19:13–26.) Be on the alert, for the devil is like a roaring lion seeking whom he can devour. Don't let him devour your heart's devotion to your God! (See 1 Peter 5:8–11.)

> Watch over your heart with all diligence, for from it flow the springs of life. (Prov. 4:23)

Please join in this prayer:

> Father, I praise and thank You for all the abundant blessings You have poured into my life. How great is Your love and how awesome Your ways. Your tender care for me is so personal, so perfect. Thank You for loving me like no other can!
>
> Yet, in spite of the beauty of Your perfect love, there are times when I doubt Your care and lose my focus. Forgive me, Lord,

for not trusting in You completely. Search my heart, and show me where I am holding onto the things that You have blessed me with. Help me release them, Lord, so that they can do the work You designed them for, in my life and in the lives of others!

Father, move throughout me to open my eyes to see the double portion that You have already blessed me with. Open my heart to respond with a resounding and continual shout of joy to Your name! Make me to be a vehicle of blessing, where no legitimate need would go unmet, no heart's cry would be unnoticed. Fill me with Your grace and power so that I may be a vehicle of blessing to all those about me! In all things, may I give You the glory and honor that is due to Your name. Move in power and might to turn all hearts toward You. Change my heart, Father, so that my response would be, "Not unto me, oh Lord, not unto me, but may all the glory go unto You!"

# 5

# A Drop in the Bucket

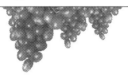

But do not let this one fact escape your notice, beloved, that with the Lord one day is like a thousand years, and a thousand years like one day. (2 Peter 3:8)

Now the boy Samuel was ministering to the Lord before Eli. And word from the Lord was rare in those days, visions were infrequent. It happened at that time as Eli was lying down in his place (now his eyesight had begun to grow dim and he could not see well), and the lamp of God had not yet gone out, and Samuel was lying down in the temple of the Lord where the ark of God was, that the Lord called Samuel; and he said, "Here I am." Then he ran to Eli and said, "Here I am, for you called me." But he said, "I did not call, lie down again." So he went and lay down. The Lord called yet again, "Samuel!" So Samuel arose and went to Eli and said, "Here I am, for you called me." But he answered, "I did not call, my son, lie down again." Now Samuel did not yet know the Lord, nor had the word of the Lord yet been revealed to him. So the Lord called Samuel again for the third time. And he arose and went to Eli and said, "Here I am, for you called me." Then Eli discerned that the Lord was calling the boy. And Eli said to Samuel, "Go lie down, and it shall be if He calls you, that you shall say, 'Speak, Lord, for Your servant is listening.'" So Samuel went and lay down in his place. Then the Lord came and stood and called as at other times, "Samuel! Samuel!" And Samuel said, "Speak, for Your servant is listening." (1 Sam. 3:1–15)

Meditations for a spiritual checkup: How often do you miss a move of God because you are expecting Him to show up today in the same way He did yesterday? If God met you only in the context of the parameters of your expectations, He would not be God but a malleable puppet whose strings you could capriciously control.

When God surprises you, will you draw in closer or will you run away? Fear of the unknown will set your feet to running, while a love-bound soul will move in closer to catch a clearer glimpse of the beloved. So how much do you really love God? The level of your love will be demonstrated by the direction your feet turn when the unexpected hits you in the face like a cold bucket of water. Will you lunge into hiding or fully cast yourself into His arms of grace?

Do you approach Him with a spirit of familiarity or with one of awe and reverence? Yes, He does call you friend. (See John 15:14–15.) You have a level of intimacy with Him that is beyond compare, but this must always be balanced with a reverential awe and fear of the Lord's majesty, greatness, and power. Anything less brings Him down to your level of humanity and robs you of seeing more of the fullness of His glory!

Do you really treat the things of God as marvelous and hold them with trembling hands at the wonder of all He has given you? Or have you grown incredibly complacent and too content? Is there a holy fire burning in your gut to see and know more of your Lord?

Do not despise the wilderness times of your life, for in them you have nowhere to go but to God. As you seek Him, He will allow you to find Him and see Him with a new, more profound depth. Your flesh will always seek after comfort, but your God will call you again and again to reach up to Him and deny yourself so you might behold more of Him and grow in your character and Christlikeness.

We are each just a drop in the bucket of life, yet God sees, God knows, and God cares about every little detail of your life. Truly we serve an awesome and mighty God! Will you turn aside to see Him more clearly?

# 6

# A Drop in the Bucket—Part 2

> But do not let this one fact escape your notice, beloved, that
> with the Lord one day is like a thousand years, and a thousand
> years like one day. (2 Peter 3:8)

A drop in the bucket is my life,
Is my life on this earth.
I will not touch millions,
Not many will know,
Few will know of my birth.

But You, dear Lord, see all my days,
You know my every thought.
You planned each moment,
Before there was one,
And none will escape Your sight.

Nothing escapes the gaze of God,
Nothing is useless or vain.
You take it all and hold it close,
And use all of my pain.
You use all of my pain.

You draw me close,
Say, "Child, come near,
There is nothing to fear.
For I have known you before time began,
And I hold your future, dear.

"I hold each day and cherish your
   thoughts,
I'll draw you close to My side.
If you will but come to Me,
And in My words abide,
And in My Word abide.

"Run quickly now while I can be found,
For soon the days will come,
When judgment will cover the earth.
The moment of recompense begun,
For those who did not turn to the Son.

"But today there is still time to come,
To seek My gracious hand.
So don't delay, but quickly run,
Into My heart of love,
Into My heart of love.

"I see it all from far above,
And yet I walk by your side.
Don't doubt, don't fear,
Don't look away,
But in My presence abide.

"For I will shelter and keep you,
Your enemies will not prevail.
I hold you closely to My side,
For it's in Me that you can hide,
In Me you can hide.

"I hold you closely to My side,
I will not let you go.
Even when through deep waters,
You flounder and lose control,
I will buoy you back up with hope.

"I am still there to hear your cries,
I feel all of your pain.
So child, turn it all to Me,
It will be for you gain,
You will heaven gain.

"I see it all from far above,
And yet I walk by your side.
Don't doubt don't fear or look away,
But in My presence abide.
In My presence abide."

# 7

# A Small God

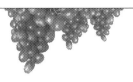

> They were utterly astonished saying, "He has done all things
> well; He makes even the deaf to hear and the mute to speak."
> (Mark 7:37)

When was the last time you were amazed by God? We are not amazed, not caught up in heavenly wonder because our concept of God is too civilized and too small!

*Your God is too small if:*

He only meets your expectations
He ceases to surprise you
His love does not delight you
And continue to amaze you
Your God is too small

*Your God is too small if:*

His justice repels you
His holiness does not draw you
His greatness is not pondered
His glory is not sought
And His care becomes mundane
Your God is too small

*Your God is too small if:*

His mercies reside in yesterday
His miracles are relegated to prior ages
His ways are explainable
His wisdom is understandable
His methods are predictable
Your God is too small

*Your God is too small if:*

His counsel is forgettable
His joy does not energize you
His covering does not draw you
His care does not impact you
His tears do not move you
Your God is too small

*Your God is too small if:*

His compassion does not flow through you
His love does not pour out of you
His gentleness does not moderate you
His wisdom does not direct you
His presence does not comfort you
Your God is too small

*Are you living with a small or a big God?*

# 8

## When Contentment Kills

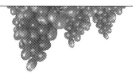

> But we had to celebrate and rejoice, for this brother of yours was dead and has begun to live, and was lost and has been found. (Luke 15:32)

> But now in Christ Jesus you who formerly were far off have been brought near by the blood of Christ. For He Himself is our peace, who made both groups into one and broke down the barrier of the dividing wall. (Eph. 2:13–14)

God has given you Jesus Himself. Do you understand the depth, power, and majesty this portrays? He alone is the peace everyone is searching after. It is found in nothing or no one but Jesus Himself. In this world you will have trouble, but take courage, for He has overcome the world. He has given you everything pertaining to holiness and righteousness; fear not. You have it all. And you are only beginning to live as you move into a deeper understanding of the fullness of God's ownership and appropriate all that Jesus has purchased for you on that terrible, wonderful cross: life, peace, mercy, grace, glory, reunion with the Father, keys to the kingdom, and coheirship. Truly all you ever need is to be found in Jesus. He has given Himself unreservedly, completely, and passionately for you. How will He also not freely give you all you need to walk in the manifestation of His glory and plan for your life?

When you come to Jesus, you have only started to live. Your residence has been transferred from the kingdom of darkness unto the kingdom of light. But this is just the beginning. Celebrate and worship God for the miraculous work He has done. This is the foundation of your new life in Christ. But in this you have only seen a snippet of God's incredible plan for your life. Your spiritual journey does not just denote a passage of time as you sojourn on this earth. It also hints at the fullness and depth of God's love that He desires to pour forth into your life. Push beyond the baby steps of salvation and reach up for all that God has planned for you since the beginning of time. Heaven forbid that you should become so comfortable in your position with Christ that you cease to hunger, thirst, and yearn for more and more of Him. *This is only the beginning of life.* Determine to move further and deeper into all that God is and all that He has planned. Contentment in this area is absolute death to experiencing more of the divine nature of your God. Reach up and cry out for more of Jesus, for a deeper revelation of His majesty and a more complete filling with His Holy Spirit.

No matter where you are in your journey with Jesus, He has so much more to give you and boundless depths to reveal to you. Will you reach up for them? Will you thirst for them like one mired in desert sand? Will you call out to Him, "Show me more of You or else I will die!" We all need a hunger that is this fervent, radical, and urgent. *Spiritual contentment kills this type of burning desire.* It is my heart's plea for God's people that He will awaken in each one of us a passion for Him that will burn with fierceness and intensity unlike anything this world has seen. Will you give your all so that Jesus can move you beyond to a deeper state of living for Him?

There are seasons when God draws you through a huge battle and calls you aside to rest. In this time He refuels, feeds, strengthens, and fortifies you. Dwell here, be sheltered in His arms, and enjoy His embrace. Rest here, dear one, and do not allow guilt and the expectations of others to pull you away from this time of intimacy with God. Yet, do not linger here beyond the time necessary to re-shine your armor. Once God has healed and mended, encouraged and equipped, step back out in faith to engage once again in the battle. Our work is not done until we see Him face to face. Do not give up. God will use your pain. He will pour into you so that you can then pour into others, and in doing so, you will behold the face of God! You will move beyond the stage of just beginning to live to embracing the fullness of the glory of God that was deposited in you on the day of your salvation. Do not waste it! Step out in faith, giving all in the name of Jesus, and know that as you pour out, God will continue to pour in. He will not leave you bereft.

# 9

# Blessings of Obedience

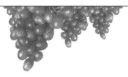

> Do you not know that when you present yourselves to someone as slaves for obedience you are slaves of the one whom you obey, either of sin resulting in death, or of obedience resulting in righteousness? But thanks be to God that though you were slaves of sin, you became obedient from the heart to that form of teaching to which you were committed, and having been freed from sin, you became slaves of righteousness. (Rom. 6:16–18)

> I am God Almighty; walk before Me and be blameless. (Gen. 17:1b)

Obedience. What picture does that word conjure up in your mind? Is it one of gritting the teeth and toughing out something you would rather not do? Is it an image of outward reluctant action? Or is it a vision of a joyful dance and opportunity to engage with the divine? Your perception of obedience is merely a picture of how you view God! Is He your taskmaster or the lover of your soul?

Our response to God's prompting in a perfect world would always be yes and amen. Yet all too often the pull of sin and the call of holiness set up a war in the spirit. When God calls, we often analyze it, turn it over, and dissect it. We impose the parameters of human understanding upon the divine missive, and in doing so, we lose the opportunity to glimpse the grandeur of heaven. As we link our darkened understanding to the movement of the Spirit, we in essence are trying to once again get God to fit in our box! God does not call us to understand but simply to trust and obey. Are we willing submit to His lordship and follow His leading? Our understanding of our God and His kingdom grows exponentially through the process of obedience! He is almighty—so why do we question the movement of His Spirit?

When we disobey, that portion of our spirit becomes like dead wood. It is unable to hear or respond to the Spirit's urging because of the self-inflicted damage caused by ignoring God's guidance and directions. The more we disobey, the more our spirits become darkened in their understanding and hampered in their ability to discern what is holy and good. Lacking this understanding, we revert to what we know, see, and understand. Our lives become once again mired in an earth-bound focus, and we lose the opportunity to dance to the cadence of heaven. It is so easy to live just for today. We become immersed in all those issues that vie for our attention, and in the process, we lose the vision of how the puzzle pieces of our lives are building our spiritual house. The most mundane things of life shape and impact our future. We build our lives moment by moment and brick by brick. Each decision we make leads us further into either the freedom of Christ or the bondage of sin.

God calls us to be trustworthy. Obedience is God's measuring tool for our level of trust. The more we trust Him, the more it will become natural to follow and obey. When we obey without trust, we are following orders as a slave would follow his master's directions. It becomes mere action, with no heart involvement. When we obey because we trust God, our joy is multiplied beyond reason. It is as if in the action of obedience we catch a deeper picture of how very much our God loves us!

As our perception of God's love grows, we realize that we are indeed sons and daughters who are heirs of His kingdom. As sons and daughters, we must walk according to the rules of the house! These rules are for our freedom and benefit. They are for our protection and direction. *Our level of obedience acts as the key to unlock the hold sin has on our spirits and sets us free to worship, adore, and reverence the King!* Each decision we make either frees us to dance in His courts or wounds us and binds our feet. Praise God for the blood of Christ! When we stumble and fall, all we need to do is call on the blood for our purification and cleansing. His blood breaks the ties that have bound our feet and frees us once again to dance with Him. He frees us to be God's tuning forks. Decision by decision, our sensitivity to His Spirit grows or diminishes. We are called to be so sensitive to a touch of His hand that as He moves, we vibrate with the glory of heaven. Are we vibrating?

> I sought the Lord, and He answered me, and delivered me from all my fears. They looked to Him and were radiant, and their faces will never be ashamed. This poor man cried and the Lord heard him and saved him out of all his troubles. The angel of the Lord encamps around those who fear Him and rescues them. (Ps. 34:4–7)

# 10

# He Holds Me Close

O LORD, You have searched me and known *me*. You know when I sit down and when I rise up; You understand my thought from afar. You scrutinize my path and my lying down, and are intimately acquainted with all my ways. Even before there is a word on my tongue, Behold, O LORD, You know it all. You have enclosed me behind and before, and laid Your hand upon me. *Such* knowledge is too wonderful for me; It is *too* high, I cannot attain to it. (Ps. 139:1–6, emphasis added)

He holds me close. My God knows me inside and out. He is ever mindful of the plans He laid for me before time began. He knows when I will follow and when I will deviate from His perfect will. He knows the intimacy of my thoughts and how deeply I rationalize my actions to myself even when I am unaware that I am doing so. He knows what darts of the Enemy can derail me, and He holds out His hand to guide me over those pitfalls. He shelters me in ways unfathomable and guides me through dangers and perils unseen and unacknowledged. He guides my foot when I think I am walking on a broad path, but in reality I am on a slippery slope just one foot fall short of plunging into despair and sin. He knows what will elicit a spirit of praise and worship with my heart. And He knows when those dark days will dampen my will to honor Him. He knows, and He still loves me.

He knows what I need and when and how I will need it. He knows what to withhold to create in me a heart that longs after Him and pursues Him with the passion of a dying man. He knows it all, and it is His pleasure to order and shape everything that impacts my life. He knows the sudden surprises that knock the breath out of me, and He sees how they will be used either to move me into a deeper state of holiness or to set me on a path of blame shifting and hiding. He knows when a gentle touch is needed. Oh, how His heart longs for a spirit within me that would be sensitive to His gentle voice! Yet He knows where I am tone deaf to Him, and He knows when and where I will choose to ignore His Word and the counsel of His Spirit and choose my own path. He knows, and He still holds me tightly in His arms of love.

He looks down on me from heaven's perspective yet is as close as my next breath. His counsel is ever open to me if I am willing to hear it. His wisdom is free for the asking. He can bandage any wound better and cleaner than any skilled physician. He uses those wounds to strengthen me and to protect me, through the lesson learned, from other pitfalls that would have been even more disastrous for my soul. How deep and broad and wide is the love of God! He hears the praise of my heart when I feel as if I would burst for the joy of His love. He hears, and His Father's heart is deeply pleased. He brings my agony of petition before the throne as the Spirit groans within me with longings too deep for words. He hears, He knows and He will answer.

As I rejoice in Him, He laughs with me and swings me by the hand as a father would play with his child. When sorrows threaten to submerge my hope, He weeps and holds out His nail-scarred hands. When I agonize over the sin and pain of others, He holds me close and whispers into my soul, "You are only beginning to experience the wonder and agony of My love for you. It is a blessed thing to share in the Father's love for another." Oh the wonder of this divine work. It takes a sin-stressed soul and creates a vessel of honor and glory and holiness that is fit for the throne room of God!

He cries out to us all, "Be ye holy as I am holy." Yet He knows that within us there is nothing resembling His utter cleanness and uprightness. We are pure before Him through the blood of Jesus, but our process of sanctification is indeed a lifelong process. As soon as we have succeeded in honoring Him with one aspect of our life, He gently and surely begins the next phase of revealing another lump of attitude that needs refining and purifying. He knows every step of the process, and through each growing pain, He holds us ever closer to His heart. If we will listen closely, we can hear Him calling, "Child, do you now understand the depth and purity of My love for you?" May our hearts ever be growing in their pursuit of His holiness and understanding of the completeness and purity of His love!

# 11

# The Sigh of Jesus

They brought to Him one who was deaf and spoke with difficulty, and they implored Him to lay His hand on him. Jesus took him aside from the crowd, by himself, and put His fingers into his ears, and after spitting, He touched his tongue with the saliva; and looking up to heaven with a deep sigh, He said to him, "Ephphatha!" that is, "Be opened!" And his ears were opened, and the impediment of his tongue was removed, and he began speaking plainly. And He gave them orders not to tell anyone; but the more He ordered them, the more widely they continued to proclaim it.
(Mark 7:32–36)

During His earthly ministry, Jesus went about healing, helping, and preaching the kingdom good news. His healing spoke to His authority and power over all illness, every evil spirit, and even death itself. His acts of healing verified both His identity as the Son of God and His divine ministry to an often spiritually deaf and blind people. It was His joy to do the will of the Father and reach out to touch those who approached Him with sincere hearts of faith. As His ministry unfolded, the crowds became thick, and demands for help were unceasing. He often drew aside from the crowd to sit in communion with God the Father in order to be equipped for the next step in His earthly journey. This displayed the unique marriage of both the human and divine nature of our Lord.

As God, Jesus knew the heart of this deaf man, and even before healing him, He knew how he would respond. It is no different today. He knows how we will handle every blessing and every trial before they cross our path. Even though Jesus warned him to remain quiet, Jesus knew that this soon-to-be-healed man would joyously proclaim his good news to anyone who would listen. Perhaps this is why He sighed. He poured out of Himself healing power to meet the needs of one who would then in his joy blatantly disobey Jesus' command to remain silent in regard to the loosening of his tongue and clearing of his ears. It was not the right time to declare the glory and healing of Jesus. Is it any different today?

When Jesus meets us in a profound way, our immediate response is often to run out and tell our nearest neighbor. Just like this man in Scripture, we want to stand on the rooftops and proclaim the good news! At times this is very appropriate, but not always. Jesus sees each piece of the puzzle, and He knows how each one needs to fit together to bring God the greatest glory. Those puzzle pieces even include the parameters and attitudes of our praise! An aptly spoken word can bring much joy and enlightenment to the hearer, but a word spoken rashly, without the leading and guidance of the Holy Spirit, can actually fall down upon the recipient's spirit like salt hitting a raw wound.

We do not know what burdens our brethren are carrying, and if we are carried away by the emotion of the moment, we will be impervious to the gentle nudges of the Spirit when He prompts us to remain silent. When we respond to a move of God with unbridled exuberance and unknowingly wound a brother or sister, God sighs. There are seasons for the outpouring of the joy welling up in our spirits, and there are times to hold them close to our hearts and ponder, like Mary, all that God has shown us. There is an appropriate time for each, and when we run ahead of God and share the fruit before it is completely ripe, we subvert the full intention God had to bring forth from that good word, kind touch, or personal revelation.

It is intensely humbling to realize that we even need to bring our praises underneath the Lordship of Jesus Christ, but why would it be any different when we have given Him everything that is in us at the moment of salvation? We are His, for He bought us with an inestimable price. He is due all of our praise and glory for now and all of eternity. Yet He also is to be Lord over the expression of our praise, whether it is held close to our hearts or shared far and wide. As in everything, we need to look to Him for guidance and listen closely to His directions. When we act purely on impulse, we set Jesus sighing once again. How I want to bring my Jesus pleasure and joy rather than cause a heavenly sigh. By God's grace, let us lean in closer to Him and listen intently to not only His directions but the heartbeat and pulse behind His instructions that always point to the immeasurable love and patience of our Father.

# 12

# The Least of These

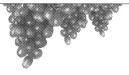

But when the Son of Man comes in His glory, and all the angels with Him, then He will sit on His glorious throne. All the nations will be gathered before Him; and He will separate them from one another, as the shepherd separates the sheep from the goats; and He will put the sheep on His right, and the goats on the left. Then the King will say to those on His right, "Come, you who are blessed of My Father, inherit the kingdom prepared for you from the foundation of the world. For I was hungry, and you gave Me something to eat; I was thirsty, and you gave Me something to drink; I was a stranger, and you invited Me in; naked, and you clothed Me; I was sick, and you visited Me; I was in prison, and you came to Me." Then the righteous will answer Him, "Lord, when did we see You hungry, and feed You, or thirsty, and give You something to drink? And when did we see You a stranger, and invite You in, or naked, and clothe You? When did we see You sick, or in prison, and come to You?" The King will answer and say to them, "Truly I say to you, to the extent that you did it to one of these brothers of Mine, even the least of them, you did it to Me." (Matt. 25:31–40)

The "least of these"—these are the ones we do not normally see. They are those precious souls who have been so battered and bruised by life that they just seem to shrink into the corners of society because they have lost their appetite to engage with the world. Their pain is palpable, honest, and raw, and we dare not get too close lest we lose our joy and become infected with their sorrow. So we minister at arm's length, never truly being willing to draw alongside them and help them shoulder their crosses. What good are warm platitudes when their souls are crying out for sustainable bread? Their souls cry, but often their voices lay dormant and silent and we are too busy to notice the difference or even to care. Then there are the others we have noticed. We reach out to share the love of God, and it falls flat. We don't know where to turn with the depth of their pain except to bring their needs to God in prayer and walk away. How well are we doing to love the least of these? Jesus calls us to carry our own load and bear others' burdens, but all too often we become so focused on our own load that we are completely out of touch with others' burdens—ouch!

We will not go the distance to love the least of these until we have partaken of a full measure of God's love. It is a love that loves best when we are at our ugliest and in our most desperate moments. It is a love that reaches down into the muck and mire of this world and gets absolutely filthy with the stench of our sin. Our Lord reaches down to meet us right where we are in the midst of all our issues, and He washes us clean with Jesus' blood. He shifts our vision from earth to heaven and empowers us with the strength of His love that cannot be quenched, extinguished, or ignored. It is not in us to love unconditionally and without reservation, but once we have tasted this type of love flowing from the Savior, we realize there is no other way to love. As we earnestly seek Him, He graciously begins the arduous task of molding and shaping our hearts into a condition that is able to receive the fullness of His grace, mercy, and love. We are helpless to love with a perfect love, but God is not. As He pours His passions into His children, we become aligned with His heartbeat for the lost and hurting.

Loving with a God-sized love may seem daunting and overwhelming at first. Yet as we seek His heart, He will fill us with His unselfish and other-centered type of love. This is the currency that will meet the needs of the least of these and bring joy to God's heart. We need to cling tightly to His hand and ask Him to help us see and perceive others from His perspective, not our own. We must begin to reach out when He provides the doorway. Our steps may be wobbly at first as we reach out to those in need, but we will find that with each faltering step, God will pour in more of His love as we pour out what little we have to love in His name. The more we pour out, the more He pours in, and His love is multiplied within us. As we begin to walk in this way, we will discover that the divine dance becomes a seamless flow of love pouring forth from heaven's throne through us to meet the needs of a terribly needy world. Then we will truly know that in loving the least of these, we have touched the heartbeat of heaven and honestly loved God.

# 13

# The Sandbox

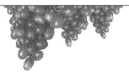

Get me out of the sandbox,
Where all I want to do is play.
Get me out of the sandbox,
Where colored toys rule the day.
Toys will break, grow old, and mold,
Fights ensue, their possessions to hold.
Get me out of the sandbox,
Where I focus on me and my habits of old.

Get me out of the sandbox,
Where the sand is pure and clean.
Get me out of the sandbox,
To a world where Your love is unseen.
Teach me to wander right where You lead,
To trust only in the move of Your hand.
Let me lead by example,
And on Your holiness only to stand.

Get me out of the sandbox,
Where other children play.
Get me out of the sandbox,
With Your fierce, fiery love for today.
It's new and fresh, moving fast as the wind,
It burns bright with Your passions within.
Get me out of the sandbox,
Fill and send me to the world for God to win.

# 14

# Our Waiting God

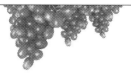

How can it be that God waits on me?

God,
He waits
He waits to hear the concerns of my heart
He waits to answer those prayers I have yet to pray
He waits to hear me ask to see more of His love and glory
He waits to forgive me for those little sins I have swept under the rug
He waits to see more of my character conform into the image of Jesus
He waits for me to ask for strength to face my current trials and situations
He waits for my branches to bear fruit as I yield the pruning's pain to Him
He waits for my passions to engage with His heart, away from my selfish
desires
He waits to hear my call for help when I refuse to solve it in my own strength
He waits to see my dreams conform slowly to the fit within His good plans
He waits to show me more of His love, if I will but ask and trust His hand
He waits for me to put aside selfish desires and motives and listen to Him
He waits for a heart willing to set aside personal plans to seek His face
He waits for me to care enough to intercede on behalf of others
He waits to hear my voice join in worship with the heavens
He waits for me to pick up my cross and follow
Still He waits
And heaven sits in silent wonder that God almighty
would wait upon His creation

Where is God waiting on you?

Or do you think lightly of the riches of His kindness and
tolerance and patience, not knowing that the kindness of God
leads you to repentance? (Rom. 2:4)

# 15

# Cost of Discipleship

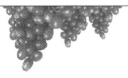

So you see a man skilled in his work? He will stand before kings, he will not stand before obscure men. (Prov. 22:29)

All that we have has been given to us by God. Any understanding, any love, fullness of devotion, and piercing of the Scriptures have all been birthed in the heart of the Father, purchased for us by the blood of the Son, and delivered unto us by the hand of the Spirit. We cannot move in a fuller spiritual fruit unless God has authored it. So why do we try to manufacture it on our own? Why do we try to polish our "Christianese" so we look good when we talk and walk among the brethren? Like chameleons, we try to blend into the atmosphere around us so we look just like the sister or brother we are walking alongside. We are to spur one another on to good works, and it is critical that we are discipled by more mature believers. We must also come alongside younger followers to encourage and teach. But this cannot be our only source of food! We must sit at the feet of the Savior and listen intently to His heart of love. We must allow Him to author and birth in us the destiny and plan He has designed for our own lives. If we only model others around us, we will never see or experience the completeness of God pouring into our own lives. We must go back to the source of the fountain: Jesus Christ Himself!

As we learn to drink more deeply of the truth and love of God, we will be transformed and changed. We will move into a fuller measure of God's indwelling glory, often without recognizing it within ourselves. We will not see the glory, but we will begin to experience a deeper ache and hunger, an undeniable passion to know more fully the glory of the Lord, just as we have been fully known. As God draws us to Himself and we begin to respond and reach up to Him, the fire of devotion will burn deeper and brighter within us. It will faithfully burn off the dross in our spirits to reveal the treasure of silver and gold hidden within. As our Father continues this polishing process, our spirits will begin to shine and radiate with the beautiful glory of God. God, in His grace, will often not reveal this to our understanding … because if we were to behold the fullness of all He is doing in us, it would tempt us to gather the praise and honor unto ourselves.

So be encouraged; when you are reaching up and when you don't feel or see His presence, He is still at work to mold and shape you into the fullness of His glory. Your pit of deepest struggle will yield the brightest and purest refining fire that will mold and shape you into the image of the risen Lord. As you continue to follow and allow the Lord to do the completeness of His work in your spirit, you will encounter a variety of responses in those around you. Some will be drawn to you because they see the fire of God within. Do not let their admiration pour into you, for it will become a cesspool in your spirit. If you gather their acclaim unto yourself, it will begin to rot and skew your focus away from God. Offer their praise as a thanks offering back unto God with the realization that anything of worth that you have done has been because of His guidance and blessing.

As God continues to change you from the inside out, others will be frightened because they see in you something they cannot comprehend. They will be mystified and often repelled because they are viewing it with earth-bound eyes. Do not turn away! If the fire of God has begun to burn bright, you must lean harder into Him and ask for His compassion and mercy to love those who are perplexed by the Jesus they see in you. Do not turn away from them, but love them unto the Lord.

God is about the work developing and honing your faith. He keeps working in each life incident and decision. As His work purifies, it will begin to develop a razor sharp faith that cuts and convicts. As you walk with Him, learn to yield all brokenness to Him for His healing and refining. The sharp sword is doing its work. As He pours forth His work from your life into others around you, at times the pureness of His actions will cut and pierce your self-righteousness, causing you to bleed in the spirit. It is His desire for this work to be unto your healing and completeness. It is for good and not for devastation. However, the enemy has so blinded the eyes of some that all they will see is carnage. Take heart; God will not leave you there, and as you pour out your brokenness to Him, He will rearrange the shards of your shattered misconceptions to draw you into the fire of His fullness and brilliance of His glory.

# 16

# Marked for a Mission

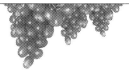

> Thus the lord used to speak to Moses face to face, just as a man speaks to his friend. When Moses returned to the camp, his servant Joshua, the son of Nun, would not depart from the tent. (Ex. 33:11)

Our God knows everything about us, and His eyes are continually searching for those who will dedicate their lives to Him. That is the crux of the matter: devoted dedication. God calls and offers the sacrifice of His Son for our healing and benefit, but few answer the call to salvation. The pathway to salvation is narrow, and a minority will find it. Even fewer hear the call of God to dance in His courts with abandoned worship and are willing to adore Him unreservedly. It is tempting to focus solely on present-day leaders who God has called to move His body of believers closer to the heartbeat of the King. Anointed servants who carry the scent of God's presence quickly catch the attention of the sheep. It is tempting to throw off all discernment and blindly follow earthly leaders because they are so available and appealing in their godly focus and attitudes. Yet when we allow our leaders to become the sole focus of our attention, we can be quickly led astray by doctrine that may be a little bit off center. In the process, we begin to gather the admiration of these leaders to our hearts rather than hungering after the God who created them. We are drinking from small side streams when we have the roaring river of God available for our refreshment and refueling!

Joshua portrays a beautiful portrait of a dedicated follower's heart. His position was to follow and serve Moses, and accordingly, he accompanied Moses to the tent of meeting. Moses entered and conversed with God on behalf of the people. God's favor rested on Moses, and here in the holy place, the divine bent down to kiss the mortal. Moses knew a level of communication with the Almighty that was so pure and profound that at one point he even had to cover his face from the people because of the glory covering him. He was a man thoroughly marked by the presence of God!

Joshua was privileged to serve God's man, and he witnessed up close how God's presence changed and empowered Moses. It would have been tempting to bow down low and reverence Moses. Most of us would have. But God had given Joshua eyes to see a little clearer and a heart to ponder the presence of God. He had glimpsed the glory of God covering Moses, and he knew it came from Moses' time both on Mount Sinai and in the tent of meeting. This birthed a hunger that was more than curiosity. It burned in Joshua's spirit as God began to plant within him a heart full of devotion and sold-out dedication. There was no turning back. Joshua had glimpsed God through Moses, and he was bold enough to want some of what Moses had gleaned. So as Moses returned to camp, Joshua stayed at the edge of the tent of meeting to seek and experience God. God was calling, and Joshua had the ears to hear and the heart to obey.

We live in an age where we are surrounded by teachers and leaders. Some flow with the full anointing of God while others are self-proclaimed shepherds. We desperately need a heart of discernment to differentiate between the two. Both look good, both sound good, and both will draw large crowds. As sheep, it is always tempting to follow the masses. Scripture is the only proven and steady sifting tool, and it has been given to us freely by a Father who loves us and who knows all the perils we will face. Their words may sound good, but do they measure up to the eternal truths of God's Word? We need the heart of Joshua. We need a heart that will lovingly follow the leaders God has sent but a spirit that will yearn after God alone. Anything else borders on idol worship.

A heart of discernment will lead us to the ones God has chosen in the midst of this generation to carry the banner of His work. These servants are marked by an aroma of heaven and singular passion that is so intense that they would be branded as unbalanced if not for the presence of God surrounding them. These are the ones who have been marked for God's mission. They are the ones who have dared to draw in closer to the throne of grace and have thrown all precaution and predictability to the wind. They may not know exactly where God is leading them, but they have caught a scent of the Almighty passing by, and they are desperate to follow it.

We have the choice to follow those ushering in the fresh winds of God or to remain with the known and familiar and safe. This is a decision that will largely determine how much fruit we gather for the kingdom. But we must select wisely, for the new and exciting is not always a move of God. It must always line up with the revealed Word of God. Its leaders must be people who have poured themselves out as drink offerings before the Lord and who are solely dedicated to following the orders of the Commander-in-Chief, Jesus. Anyone else will surely lead us astray, no matter how good he or she sounds or smooth he or she talks. Those marked with the mission of God will bear the bruises of deep wrestling and countless conversations with God. No one else will have developed the mettle of spirit to lead God's people into His chosen paths. Who are we following?

# 17

# Lonely Leadership

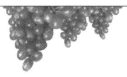

I am the Good Shepherd; the Good Shepherd lays down His life for the sheep. He who is a hired hand, and not a shepherd, who is not the owner of the sheep, sees the wolf coming, and leaves the sheep and flees, and the wolf snatches them and scatters them. He flees because he is a hired hand and is not concerned about the sheep. (John 10:11–13)

I am telling the truth in Christ, I am not lying, my conscience testifies with me in the Holy Spirit, that I have great sorrow and unceasing grief in my heart. For I could wish that I myself were accursed, separated from Christ for the sake of my brethren, my kinsmen according to the flesh, who are Israelites, to whom belongs the adoption as sons, and the glory and the covenants and the giving of the Law and the temple service and the promises, whose are the fathers, and from whom is the Christ according to the flesh, who is over all, God blessed forever. Amen. (Rom. 9:1–5)

But now, if You will, forgive their sin—and if not, please blot me out from Your book which You have written. (Ex. 32:32)

True leadership requires a great deal of sacrifice and commitment. It is not a proverbial bed of roses. It is not a roadway lined with glittering fame. A genuine leader has at all times the best interest of his people at the center of his motives, and it is the primary focus of his attention. This is no get-rich-quick scheme, nor is it a cry for notoriety or prosperity. It is completely aligning oneself with the heartbeat of Jesus. All personal comfort, self-interest, and visions of advancement are laid on the altar of God as self is sacrificed for the benefit of those served. When a true leader is born, advancement and identity are sacrificed on the altar of self. What remains is a heart completely and totally dedicated to God, even to the point of offering all of himself and even his salvation to gain the benefit and salvation of those he serves. Where are these true biblical leaders? This mindset resolutely embraces the model Christ set before us as He willingly hung on the cross to bear the burden of our sin. We claim to be Christ followers. Does His love run so deep throughout the course of our souls that we cry with this type of passion to win the lost and refine the saints?

Biblical leadership is a solitary walk that few understand and even fewer will embrace, for after all, we are sheep in need of a shepherd. We tend to wander in the same direction as the rest of the flock. Praise God for His shepherd's hook in the form of His Word spoken through His servant leaders! No wonder God calls them to stand and be courageous. He calls, "Do not fear. He who is in you is greater than he who is in the world!" (See 1 John 4:4.) Those who respond to this call have all the resources of heaven before them and the target of the enemy upon their backs. Praise God that He is both our front and rear guard!

No one but God can understand the weight of glory and purity of a God-birthed passion that covers the shoulders of His leaders. They labor long and hard with God in the secret place of the spirit to be equipped to minister to the saints and preach with the unbridled power of the gospel. True leaders lay everything at the altar of God again and again to receive what they need to benefit the people. It is often a very painful place, for God calls them to walk leading His people with a shepherd's heart—a heart willing to battle the forces that would lead them astray.

Ever-encroaching mists of deceit threaten to overwhelm and discourage God's people. These forces derail the lost and keep them enshrouded in lies that bind them in the enemy's camp. Our leaders are battling these mists every moment of every day. They train their ears to hear from the throne room and have reined in their earthly pursuits for the passion of heaven. Their knees are worn and their hearts are revived from battling in the prayer room. They carry about them the pure aroma of Jesus at great personal cost. Only a purer vision of Jesus will keep them steadfast. They have traded all of earth's glittering fame for the simple robes of a servant leader. Do we, the sheep, understand the immense call God has placed on their spirits? Will we run into our own rooms of intercession to uphold and support those who lead us to the throne of grace? Isn't it time to start?

# 18

# Who Will Hear?

As they were speaking to the people, the priests and the captain of the temple guard and the Sadducees came up to them, being greatly disturbed because they were teaching the people and proclaiming in Jesus the resurrection from the dead. And they laid hands on them and put them in jail until the next day, for it was already evening. But many of those who had heard the message believed; and the number of the men came to be about five thousand. (Acts 4:1–5)

Jerusalem, Jerusalem, who kills the prophets and stones those who are sent to her! How often I wanted to gather your children together, the way a hen gathers her chicks under her wings, and you were unwilling. Behold, your house is being left to you desolate! (Matt. 23:37–38)

For I could wish that I myself were accursed, separated from Christ for the sake of my brethren (Rom. 9:3a)

Often our present-day efforts at evangelism see limited results. Where is the move of God drawing hundreds and thousands to bend their knees to Christ in one day? The gospel was preached with immense power through mere men in Acts. We speak the same message; why are the winds of revival not sweeping the nation? Could it be because of our heart focus?

We preach from a position of comfort and security. We who have embraced the cross know there is nothing that can separate us from the love of God. We are His and He is ours, and we rejoice in our sonship. Yet God's heartbeat is to go out and search for the one lost sheep. This was also the disciples' passion. Paul's heart beat so passionately for the salvation of his brethren that if it had been possible, he was willing to lay down his own salvation to draw them into the kingdom. Do we love the lost with this type of passion? Will we allow God to move in our hearts so that we will weep with this intensity to win them into the kingdom? I wonder at the purity, passion, and complete self-denial of such an abandoned heart's focus. I treasure my salvation so deeply that it is hard to imagine being willing to yield it on the altar to win some with the message of the cross. This heart, in its purest form, is the true embodiment of the gospel message. This is indeed a God-sized love where few are willing to dwell.

The spiritual forces at work within the deceived are no match for God's immense power and grace. The battle is the same as in the days of Acts. However, now biblical literature and information floods the marketplace in all forms of media. Has their ready accessibility dampened our urgency to go out and meet the people in the street? We have grown somewhat complacent and completely comfortable within our fellowship of the saints. When we witness, it is often from a sense of obligation or fledgling love. We still have so far to go to adopt a heart that weeps with the passion and purity of Jesus as He looks out over all those yet to come to saving grace.

Do we love with such an abandon that we would, like Paul, almost wish to give up our own salvation for the benefit of another? This is truly giving one's life for not only a friend but also for one who is presently an enemy of the cross. We are completely powerless to love with this intensity. It must be birthed in the throne room of God. It is His very heartbeat. Are we willing to pick up our cross and follow Jesus once again to Golgotha? Will we be marked as people who sorrow with God over the brokenness of our world? Perhaps once God matures our love to make us more completely like Jesus, we will once again see waves of salvation wash over our land. In the meantime, reach up to heaven and cry out for a heart that loves like Jesus. You will be amazed at how your life's focus and heart's mission will change. Will we trust Him with the focus of our heart's passions?

# 19

# Battle on the Front Lines

Consider it all joy, my brethren, when you encounter various trials, knowing that the testing of your faith produces endurance. And let endurance have its perfect result, so that you may be perfect and complete, lacking in nothing. But if any of you lacks wisdom, let him ask of God, who gives to all generously and without reproach, and it will be given to him. But he must ask in faith without any doubting, for the one who doubts is like the surf of the sea, driven and tossed by the wind. For that man ought not to expect that he will receive anything from the Lord, being a double-minded man, unstable in all his ways. (James 1:2–8)

Has life thrown you a curve ball? Did the ugliness of misfortune or sin slap you in the face and leave you breathless with shock and surprise? Have you been shaken so hard that all you can see are the barren spots in your soul? Is despair staring you point blank in the face?

It is in these moments that your resolve and the mettle of your faith are truly tested. God is still good; will you believe this? Turn to Him in your angst and sorrow and you will find Him just waiting to comfort and provide for you. Yet as you move further into your love dance with your Savior, He may begin to speak words to your heart that mystify and challenge you to reach up and beyond yourself. As you journey through the stress, clinging to Him, He begins to speak: "Minister and serve through the pain, or it will consume you."

When you contemplate these words, it becomes evident that the episode of grief can cause you to become self-centered and quickly lead down the path into a pity party. When you serve from a position of deep pain and hurt, you have no resources, no strength, and often no emotion or will to pour out. It is in this place where you must totally cast yourself upon the Lord almighty. Trust Him for your every provision, your every move, your every prayer because in yourself there is nothing left to give … but for God. God's resources never run dry. He is never without a plan, a purpose, or provision. He will not leave or desert you but will fill you up with a completeness that you would have not known had it not been for the pain.

Be careful, though, that you do not become a self-appointed martyr; for even here you will be tempted to pour out of your woundedness before you have let God pour into you. If you are serving only from your position of pain, all that will emanate from your soul is a kinship of sorrow. There is no strength, no hope, and no glory because you have not put the pain on the altar of sacrifice and given God total control. This process does not happen overnight. It is a continual yielding, a constant cry for more of God's help and mercy and grace. Yet the deeper the need, the wider and greater you will come to know the heart of the Father. Along the way He tells you to pour out what He has poured in. Others will begin to see the light and hope within as you cling to God for your every breath. You begin to become less—finally! God's grace becomes bigger and greater and purer within you. Do not hide this light under the bushel! Even from the depth of your pain, God can strengthen you to minister to others who are just beginning to enter their season of wilderness. Do not lose hope, dear one. God will turn your mourning into dancing and your sorrow into joy. If you will lean hard into Him, you will begin to truly know the heart of the Father, and the hope born in this process can never be taken away!

Commit yourself to the LORD; let Him deliver him; let Him rescue him, because He delights in him. (Ps. 22:8)

Delight yourself in the LORD; and He will give you the desires of your heart. (Ps. 37:4)

Why do you spend money for what is not bread, and your wages for what does not satisfy? Listen carefully to Me, and eat what is good, and delight yourself in abundance.
(Isa. 55:2)

"Because of the iniquity of his unjust gain I was angry and struck him; I hid My face and was angry, and he went on turning away, in the way of his heart. I have seen his ways, but I will heal him; I will lead him and restore comfort to him and to his mourners, Creating the praise of the lips. Peace, peace to him who is far and to him who is near," Says the LORD, "and I will heal him." (Isa. 57:17–19)

# 20

# The Valley

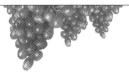

Yea, though I walk through the valley of the shadow of death
Thou wilt heal and help me
Help me
You know all my ways and You see all my days
And You call me back to Your side
You say, "Don't fear, for in Me I am calling,
Calling You to abide
Come close now, and draw to My side
My child, My love, how far you have run
You've gone your own path and moved away from My Son
Your plans wither, slowly they dry up like chaff
Come quickly now, child, to be led by My staff,
My staff"

Yea, though I walk through the valley of the shadow of death
Thou art with me to guide me and give me my breath
Thou art with me
You counsel me, "Fear not," You hold my life in Your hands
And in all to trust You even when I don't understand
The mists, they draw closer and cloud up my sight
My heart is heavy without Your delight
I've wandered away from Your side and Your heart
My pathway I chose, and from You I did depart
Please draw me back to Your side
To Your side

Yea, though I walk through the valley of the shadow of death
Your hand stretches out, my steps to gently guide
Guide me
In this valley of doubt, fear, confusion, and pain
You call me, "Dear child, I will renew you again
And align your wandering heart to draw to My side
I have so much more for you, come quickly abide
In Me, dear child, I'll shelter and shield
You away from the tumult that causes mind-numbing fear
It slows your growth, which I've planned for you, dear
Planned and designed"

Yea, though I walk through the valley of the shadow of death
I can hear Your sweet voice calling out to me
Calling
The Spirit urges me to turn now and run to see
That You're drawing me closer to eternity
With each step I hear You calling me home
You remind me often my life's not my own
It's been bought with a price so precious and pure
And anchors my steps in a love that is sure
You call, "Turn now, child, quickly to Me
And you will mount up with wings of the eagles above
And soar on the heights and wonder of love
The wonder of love"

Yea, though I walk through the valley of the shadow of death
The mists part slowly, and You guide my each step
All my steps
You hold me close now and comfort my heart
And tell me, "Child, I've seen it all right from the start
And used it all completely, not one thing's been lost
As I shape you and mold you through tempest
Where you are thoroughly tossed
I use it all, dear one, your heart to align
With My plan so simple, profound. and divine
So divine"

Yea, though I walk through the valley of the shadow of death
I now will fear not, for I've seen God's very best
Seen the best
That the Savior holds outstretched in His hand for me
I no longer need to run; He's set me completely free
From all fear, doubt, despair, and pain
He's there—He's used it to bring me His gain
He whispers my name and draws me close
He counsels me in the night watch from above
He sends His Helper to guide and to love
To love

Yea, though I walk through the valley of the shadow of death
I've come to see clearly now the thing was of me
Of me
It clouded my vision and bound my feet fast
I ran blindly ahead, but in this race I won't last
When my goal was my own and on my skills I relied
My pride grew big like a wart, ugly and plain
His ways and counsel I did openly disdain
I fell bruised and bloody, oh how could it be
That these dreams now lie empty
Abandoned and rejected, I feel so dejected
Because they were centered on me
All about me

Yea, though I walk through the valley of the shadow of death
The cross's shadow covers my shame and pain
My shame
It heals broken hearts and sets them right again
He is cleansing and pruning until all I can see
Is Jesus and His wounds suffered for me
And how He bled and died, though free from sin,
All so He could draw me completely in
He embraced death and yielded His Spirit for me
All to finally and fully set me free
Set me free from me

Yea, though I walk through the valley of the shadow of death
His wonders amazing, His plan is the best
The best
This world sees not and seems not to care
But I've come to hunger, to seek, and to strive
For that which is better than where I did hide
He's opening His heart to truths from above
So wondrous and amazing, He sent down the dove
To anoint and fill me and lead me on
And turn my heart to Jesus more clearly to see
Jesus to see

Yea, though I walk through the valley of the shadow of death
I now hear, "Friend, fear not and follow Me
Follow Me"
He calls me friend, how can it be?
That the one who was far off
Though cleansed by the blood
Has returned now to love the portals above
Aligned with heaven's heartbeat
And God calls me friend
He knows my beginning and my end
And will not desert or leave me alone
He seeks and He saves and He sifts His own
He sifts His own

Yea, though I walk through the valley of the shadow of death
I'm beginning to shine more with every breath
Every breath
Because I breathe holy air sent from the throne
My life is all His, it not is my own
I've chosen His call to follow and heed
He's promised me now to meet every need
Because I've given it all for the sake of the cross
Everything else I must count as loss
All but Jesus is loss
For Him
For Jesus alone

*His staff draws me to His side so I can see His plans and designs. Oh, the wonder of His love! It's a divine love that teaches me my life is not about me. He sets me free from me so that Jesus is all I see. He sifts His own until all I desire is Jesus alone.*

(These statements are a combination of the last lines of each verse in the poem. Can you hear God's heart?)

# 21

## Your Glory Fall Down

Let Your glory fall down, dear Lord.
Let Your glory fall down.
Oh, open our eyes that we may see.
Cleanse our hearts for Your glory,
And move on our spirits to know You.
Oh, let Your glory fall down!

Let Your glory fall down, dear Lord.
Let Your glory fall down.
We're thirsty and dying outside of Your hand.
We made a mess of this sweet land.
We've run, we've hidden from Your dear plan.
Oh Lord, let Your glory fall down!

Let Your glory fall down, dear Lord.
Let Your glory fall down.
We will not seek or thirst for You,
Unless You come and move.
Please light a fire that has grown dim,
And move us to dance with Your Spirit within.
Oh Lord, let your glory fall down!

Let Your glory fall down, dear Lord.
Let Your glory fall down.
Your people perish for lack of Your Word.
They stumble and fall because they've not heard,
The sweet and clear voice of their Lord.
Forgive us, dear Daddy, for dancing with the world.
Come cleanse and renew us within!

*Jan Hegelein*

Let Your glory fall down, dear Lord.
Let Your glory fall down.
We see so dimly, the fire is banked,
Oh Lord, sweep through and fill our tanks!
We need to hear we're desperate for You,
So lead and speak and draw us through.
Dear Father, please come!

Let Your glory fall down, dear Lord.
Let Your glory fall down.
If You light the fuse, then we truly will burn,
With a holy fire and sin will be spurned.
The dross will burn off as we truly learn,
To let Your glory fall down!

Let Your glory fall down, dear Lord.
Let Your glory fall down.
Please come now, sweet Jesus, and fill our hearts.
We need to turn and make a fresh start,
To follow and worship the only one true.
But we cannot until You draw us anew,
Draw us through Your Son!

Let Your glory fall down, dear Lord.
Let Your glory fall down.
Oh, open our eyes that we may see,
Cleanse our hearts for Your glory.
Move on our spirits to know You more,
Help us to love You and adore.
Oh, let Your glory fall down!

# 22

# Daily Bread

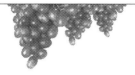

"So do not be like them; for your Father knows what you need before you ask Him. Pray, then, in this way: "Our Father who is in heaven, Hallowed be Your name. Your kingdom come, Your will be done, on earth as it is in heaven. Give us this day our daily bread. And forgive us our debts, as we also have forgiven our debtors. And do not lead us into temptation, but deliver us from evil. For Yours is the kingdom and the power and the glory forever. Amen." (Matt. 6:8–13)

There is so much food in this prayer, yet we miss most of it because of its familiarity. Look at the phrase "daily bread." What is Jesus speaking of here? Immediately our minds drift to the physical bread that sustains our bodies. We are immersed in the needs of the moment and are well acquainted with the fuel our bodies crave for survival. This is an integral part of life as we partake of physical nourishment several times daily. It is easy to assume God is talking about the need for food. On the surface, this addresses our dependence on God's generosity to provide the proper soil, sun, rain, etc., to produce the meals we so enjoy. But could there be something more to our daily bread? Since Jesus is called the Bread of Life, I believe this also refers to the spiritual food we need to sustain and grow our spirits. Both types of daily bread are essential for our wellbeing. We run quickly to the kitchen table. Do we move as fast to open the Word of God and feast on His nourishing words?

We need to ask Him daily, hourly, and each moment to give us our spiritual food. We desperately need to sit at His feet and bow low in humility before our King. We would do well to study Mary as she wiped Jesus' dusty feet with her tears and her hair. (See John 12:3.) She was willing to bend down low to worship and serve the Lord. As we truly abide with Jesus, our hearts will grow in wonder and abandonment at the beauty and greatness of His nature. Our faces will truly become "dusty" from sitting at His feet, and in the process we will shine with the glory of God!

Have you eaten of the living bread today? Is your face dusty? Have you drawn so close to Jesus that the dust from His sandals has settled on your spirit? Do you carry about you the aroma of Jesus? The Lord tells us we are the aroma of life to life and death to death. Everywhere we go, we carry within us the glory and the story of Jesus' death and resurrection. We are a living testimony to the power of the blood of Christ. Truly, at the name of Jesus everyone will one day bow and confess that He is God! But for now we are His representatives. When we go forth in His power and with the might of His presence, we will begin to see fortresses crumble and spirits soften to the love of God. The more time we spend with Him, the more we will radiate with the power of His presence and the more odiferous we will become with the glory of God! Is your face dusty from worshiping at the feet of the Savior? Yesterday's bread has already been consumed and processed. It was for yesterday. Are you feeding on fresh bread?

> Lord, cause us to hunger more for the bread of heaven than we hunger for physical food and the comforts of earth. Create in us a deep, consistent hunger for more and more of You. Forgive us, Lord, for not hungering more after You. Lord, increase our hunger for *You*!

(This is a dangerous and extremely fulfilling prayer—one that, when pursued, will cause one to both be filled and also never satisfied this side of heaven!)

Pray the Lord's Prayer, and let the depth and fullness of its meaning soak into your spirit and encourage your heart.

Our Father
Who art in heaven
Hallowed be Thy name
Thy kingdom come
Thy will be done

On earth as it is in heaven
*Give us this day our daily bread*
And forgive us our trespasses
As we forgive those who trespass against us
And lead us not into temptation
But deliver us from evil
For Thine is the kingdom
And the power
And the glory forever, Amen

Notice the first seven lines end with "our daily bread." The opening section of this prayer deals with our spiritual needs and relationship to the Father. The second half of the prayer directly follows "give us this day our daily bread" and deals with God's kingdom being established through us here on earth. We cannot access any heavenly treasure God has in store for us if we do not come to Him through the shed blood of Jesus. His will can only be done here on earth as it is done in heaven to the extent that we depend on and lean into the grace of Jesus, our daily bread. Notice also that we can't move into the part that deals with God's kingdom moving through us on earth until we have partaken of the spiritual bread (Jesus), the one who satisfies us, fuels us, and shows us the Father!

> Our fathers ate the manna in the wilderness; as it is written, "HE GAVE THEM BREAD OUT OF HEAVEN TO EAT." Jesus then said to them, "Truly, truly, I say to you, it is not Moses who has given you the bread out of heaven, but it is My Father who gives you the true bread out of heaven. For the bread of God is that which comes down out of heaven, and gives life to the world." Then they said to Him, "Lord, always give us this bread." Jesus said to them, "I am the bread of life; he who comes to Me will not hunger, and he who believes in Me will never thirst." (John 6:31–36)

> "Truly, truly, I say to you, he who believes has eternal life. I am the bread of life. Your fathers ate the manna in the wilderness, and they died. This is the bread which comes down out of heaven, so that one may eat of it and not die. I am the living bread that came down out of heaven; if anyone eats of this bread, he will live forever; and the bread also which I will give

for the life of the world is My flesh." Then the Jews therefore began to argue with one another, saying, "How can this man give us His flesh to eat?" So Jesus said to them, "Truly, truly, I say to you, unless you eat the flesh of the Son of Man and drink His blood, you have no life in yourselves. He who eats My flesh and drinks My blood has eternal life, and I will raise him up on the last day. For My flesh is true food, and My blood is true drink. He who eats My flesh and drinks My blood abides in Me, and I in him. As the living Father sent Me, and I live because of the Father, so he who eats Me, he also will live because of Me. This is the bread which came down out of heaven; not as the fathers ate and died; he who eats this bread will live forever." (John 6:47–58)

# 23

# Five Thousand Fed

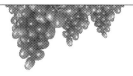

The apostles gathered together with Jesus; and they reported to Him all that they had done and taught. And He said to them, "Come away by yourselves to a secluded place and rest a while." (For there were many people coming and going, and they did not even have time to eat.) They went away in the boat to a secluded place by themselves. The people saw them going, and many recognized them and ran there together on foot from all the cities, and got there ahead of them. When Jesus went ashore, He saw a large crowd, and He felt compassion for them because they were like sheep without a shepherd; and He began to teach them many things. When it was already quite late, His disciples came to Him and said, "This place is desolate and it is already quite late; send them away so that they may go into the surrounding countryside and villages and buy themselves something to eat." But He answered them, "You give them something to eat!" And they said to Him, "Shall we go and spend two hundred denarii on bread and give them something to eat?" And He said to them, "How many loaves do you have? Go look!" And when they found out, they said, "Five, and two fish." And He commanded them all to sit down by groups on the green grass. They sat down in groups of hundreds and of fifties. And He took the five loaves and the two fish, and looking up toward heaven, He blessed the food and broke the loaves and He kept giving them to the disciples to set before them; and He divided up the two fish among them all. They all ate and were satisfied, and they picked up twelve full baskets of the broken pieces, and also

of the fish. There were five thousand men who ate the loaves.
(Mark 6:30–44)

Imagine this scene: Five thousand men filled the hillside, hungry for a touch and a word from the Master. Here was one who held all eternity in His hands, His teaching was unlike that of the Pharisees and religious leaders. It was simple and understandable yet immensely profound, and it stirred the waters of their souls. The more He spoke, the more they hungered for a touch of His righteousness, of His wisdom, and of His healing hand. Here was one with the answers—one who, by His touch, His word, His look, could heal and set things right. So they stayed. Throughout the heat and in spite of the vastness of the crowd with its throbbing force yearning to come close to the Teacher, they stayed. Despite the discomfort and unlikely possibility of getting close to Jesus in that immense crowd and in spite of growing hunger pangs, they stayed.

There is a subtle reproof for us here. Will we stay at the feet of Jesus? When things become uncomfortable, inconvenient, and downright bothersome and disruptive, will we remain focused on our Lord or go running to alleviate whatever is disturbing us? Will we remain firm in our commitment and continue to look unto our precious Jesus to meet all of our needs and our heart longings? Or will we go running away from the spiritual hillside where He will teach us and retreat once again into our cocoon of comfort and ease? Will we stay the course until we receive a touch of our dear Master's hand?

This in itself is a mighty challenge to stay focused on our Lord. Yet if we dig a bit deeper, there is another truth (actually many challenging, life-changing truths) that will challenge how we think and perceive our dear Jesus. Notice Jesus' words, "How many loaves do you have? Go look!" He already knew, but He also knew that the disciples' hearts were not quite prepared to receive the miracle He had purposed to do. So He sent them out into the crowd to take inventory.

This was no quick camera shot or Internet survey. Those disciples had to be hungry. They had to get up and begin to move throughout the crowd to seek out any source of food. Imagine their disappointment when they returned to Jesus to report a total of five loaves and two fish. How incredulous they must have felt as they pondered the idea of feeding such a mass of people with almost nothing at their disposal. How their hearts must have been pounding out the rhythm: impossible, unthinkable, ridiculous, impossible! Can you hear their heartbeat and the scream of their thinking: Jesus, send them away. We can't do this thing You ask. It is impossible!

Yes, Jesus knew. The Creator of the universe knew. He knew their heart condition, the people's hunger, and His power to meet the needs of both. So He sent them into the crowd to take inventory—not because He needed to know what the provisions were but because He was teaching the disciples to look at the need around them and to open their spiritual eyes to see that there was absolutely no way the needs of the people could be met. Not until they realized their utter hopelessness and helplessness would Jesus act. *Their plea of desperation actually prepared the platform for the unfolding miracle.* Not until the disciples realized that they were totally dependent on the grace of God would Jesus act. So He sent them out into the crowd that they might see and truly know from where their help would come. Is it any different today? As we desire to see mountains moved and road blocks of impossibility destroyed, God will often wait until our hearts are tilled and prepared to see that He is the only way!

So where do we look for help? Let us cast all of our burdens at the feet of our precious Lord, for He truly does care for us. As we draw near to Him, we will begin to see Him more clearly, and He will draw near to us. Maybe, just maybe, as we begin to refuse to trust our resources and lean harder into our Lord, we too will begin to see the glory of our God descend in this generation and His miraculous power pour forth to sustain His people and draw many forth into the kingdom before it is too late. Join with me in this plea: "Come quickly, Lord Jesus. We have no hope outside of You!"

# 24

# Exceeding Abundance

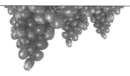

> Now to Him who is able to do far more abundantly beyond all we ask or think, according to the power that works within us, to Him be glory in the church and in Christ Jesus to all generations, forever and ever. Amen. (Eph. 3:20–21)

Who—who is this? None other than God Himself, the one—the only one—who is able.

What—what does He concern Himself with? Our thoughts and words, our hopes and dreams.

When—when does He move on our behalf? Every moment of each day. When our thoughts rush around in our heads, it is both a comfort and conviction to know that our precious Lord knows each and every one. Even before the words are formed and they barely exist in thought form, He knows them and is able to give in accordance with what we ask or think!

Where—where does He move? In our spirit man brought to life by the matchless blood of Jesus. His presence and provision are poured into our spirits and fleshed out in the world.

How—how does He move? By the matchless power and might of an almighty God through the working of the Holy Spirit within us

Why—why would He do this? He loves us and desires to reveal a deeper and fuller understanding of the completeness of God's glory so that His children will move into a deep and contagious worship!

The depth and riches these verses present are almost too much for our human minds to grasp. He is able. Our God is all powerful, all present, all knowing, all encompassing, and all loving. He possesses all wisdom, the wisdom far beyond *all* the ages of man. Only He is able to fill us with all the fullness of God and answer every heart's plea. Not only does He answer the cry at its surface value, but He also gives so much more and goes so much deeper. He gives exceedingly abundantly beyond all we can ask or think. (See Eph. 3:20.) Am I praying for my children, my family, my church, my neighbors, my community, and my nation? As God's power moves into these lives in response to my heart's cry, He works to shape them into the image of Jesus. Not only are they changed, but the generations following them will also be impacted because they were touched by the love of Jesus. Each one matters to God! Now that is definitely more than I could ask or think when I first began to pray.

God loves to pour His grace and provision upon His children. How much He wants to give us the fullness of His heart and passions. He hears the cry of our heart, and He will answer far more abundantly than we can ever hope to dream. So how big are your dreams? What are you hoping for? Where do you pin your dreams? Are they aspirations that glorify God? You can never outdo God. No dream is too big, no hope too grand. There is nothing—let me say it again—*nothing* that is outside the scope of God's love and power. So what are you dreaming for today? The salvation of a loved one? God can do that. Direction for the future? God can do that. Peace for a troubled soul? God can do that. The explosion of the gospel to win souls? God can do that. He desires to do that!

Truly, unless we abide with Jesus, we would not hope or dream for any of these things. But as we abide in Him, God puts the seed of that hope in our hearts. If He has planted that seed, surely He can water it, weed it, and cause it to grow, all according the magnificent power of the Holy Spirit who dwells within us. Praise God, He will never leave us nor forsake us, and He has left us a Helper in the form of His Spirit. So go forward in faith, dream *big* dreams, and hope yet in the Lord, for He will not disappoint!

> And my God will supply all your needs according to His riches in glory in Christ Jesus. (Phil. 4:19)

> If you abide in Me, and My words abide in you, ask whatever you wish, and it will be done for you. (John 15:7)

Oh precious Father, thank You for Your incredible love and mercy, Your sweet peace and strength, and the glories of Your outstretched arm to save. Thank you that You would even meet me in the place of my dreams, in that place of secret hope, and encourage me to run to You with those things. This is so much more than I could ever hope for, yet You go even further and give so much more—more than I could ever hope to ask or think. You fill me with the love of Christ and the fullness of God. How can this be? Thank You, dear Father, for loving me so very much and drawing my heart into unison with Your heartbeat. Thank You for moving to draw me into Your embrace and turning my eyes and my heart toward You! How great and fathomless is Your incredible love! Dearest Father, I give You all that I am, all that I think and hope, and ask You to change me and conform the innermost part of my being to reflect Your love, Your compassion, and Your mercy to the world around me. Fill me to overflowing with Your love, that it would just pour forth and bless all those You allow me to touch. Help me to dream kingdom dreams that will impact generations to come, knowing that as I have the courage to dream those dreams that You will indeed give me exceeding abundantly above all that I can ask or think. And may it all be to the glory and praise of my King!

Amen.

# 25

# Gracious God

"Also the foreigners who join themselves to the LORD, to minister to Him, and to love the name of the LORD, to be His servants, everyone who keeps from profaning the Sabbath and holds fast My covenant; even those I will bring to My holy mountain and make them joyful in My house of prayer. Their burnt offerings and their sacrifices will be acceptable on My altar; for My house will be called a house of prayer for all the peoples." The Lord GOD, who gathers the dispersed of Israel, declares, "Yet others I will gather to them, to those already gathered." (Isa. 56:6–8)

If we were to fully grasp the magnitude of God's love, we would truly be overcome. We who were filthy foreigners have been brought near to the throne of grace by the matchless, purifying blood of Jesus. It was the only way. Our God looked down on our sorry state and had mercy upon us. We who were known not, esteemed not, and had no merit within ourselves have been joined together with God's people. We have been given the privilege to worship at the holy mountain. Through the blood, we are called coheirs and righteous disciples. But are we taking the bread out of the mouths of the chosen ones? We so enjoy the pleasure of our King and all the rights and honor that go along with being part of His household. But do we remain in this state of luxuriating in His incredible arms of love? There are others who still need to be called, and the people whom He has chosen since the time of Abraham still walk in darkness and despair of soul. Do we truly care?

God holds Israel close to His heart. Will we do the same? Will we boldly enter our rooms of prayer and lift our hearts from our personal concerns to stand in the gap and intercede for the provision, safety, and salvation of God's chosen people? God promises to bless those who bless Israel, so why would we want to deny ourselves of God's blessing? This may be an initial motive, but as we move forward to pray in obedience, God will tweak our affections to love as He loves. How we need a fresh wind to blow throughout our spirits to position and align us with the Father's heart! It all starts with a blatantly honest admission of our heart's condition and lack of love. How well we know that our hearts are deceitful, and we in and of ourselves cannot truly know all that resides within. Praise God! He is so willing to sift us like wheat! He will remove all the impurities and shape within us a spirit that is more closely aligned to His heart, if we will ask.

The one who asks must be willing to put his hand to the plow and not look back. We must count the cost. Are we willing to sacrifice personal comfort and ease to join with the heartbeat of heaven? Will we allow God to break our hearts with what breaks His? It is when we are willing to truly be broken and poured out that we will find the greatest mystery of all: the matchless and limitless sufficiency of God. It is so easy to give mental assent to the complete fullness of our God. Do we live in the manifestation of that fullness? It starts with a follower who has discovered the joys of serving God with humility and integrity. When we are truly willing to reflect the glory for everything back to God, He reaches down in love and mercy and realigns our hearts and passions.

Almost unseen by our own hearts, God begins to pour forth a new mission, love, and direction when we call out, "Here I am Lord, use me." (See Isa. 6:8) It is a call of willingness, with no reservations, conditions, or predetermined parameters. It is yielding all of our dreams, hopes, and aspirations to the one who designed us in the first place! As Creator, He sees where and how we will fit into His kingdom's plans the best. Once again our sole job is to follow just as we did at the moment of salvation. It is both simple and complex, but it is a daily call. Lay down ambition, pick up the cross, and follow Jesus. As we walk in this surrender with increasingly devoted hearts, we will begin to see Him more fully and begin to glimpse the completeness of the Father's heart of love.

> Jesus got up and went away from there to the region of Tyre. And when He had entered a house, He wanted no one to

know of it; yet He could not escape notice. But after hearing of Him, a woman whose little daughter had an unclean spirit immediately came and fell at His feet. Now the woman was a Gentile, of the Syrophoenician race. And she kept asking Him to cast the demon out of her daughter. And He was saying to her, "Let the children be satisfied first, for it is not good to take the children's bread and throw it to the dogs." But she answered and said to Him, "Yes, Lord, but even the dogs under the table feed on the children's crumbs." And He said to her, "Because of this answer go; the demon has gone out of your daughter." (Mark 7:24–29)

For Zion's sake I will not keep silent, and for Jerusalem's sake I will not keep quiet, until her righteousness goes forth like brightness, and her salvation like a torch that is burning. (Isa. 62:1)

# 26

# Image Bearer

> Ah Lord GOD! Behold, You have made the heavens and the earth by Your great power and by Your outstretched arm! *Nothing is too difficult for You*, who shows lovingkindness to thousands, but repays the iniquity of fathers into the bosom of their children after them, O great and mighty God The LORD of hosts is His name; great in counsel and mighty in deed, whose eyes are open to all the ways of the sons of men, giving to everyone according to his ways and according to the fruit of his deeds; who has set signs and wonders in the land of Egypt, and even to this day both in Israel and among mankind; and *You have made a name for Yourself,* as at this day. (Jer. 32:17–21, emphasis added)

How is God making a name for Himself in you? He is deeply invested in you and watches over you with a caring love that is deeper than the oceans themselves. Do you see and know how much He loves you? In His arms of love there is comfort, but there is also a conforming, shaping, and molding that will take place if you are truly a disciple of Jesus. He does not leave you alone as an orphan but deals with you as a son or daughter. Sometimes He moves in affirmation and others in discipline. His ministrations move in conjunction with the heart's state and condition. If you are currently being tweaked in your spirit, it is merely evidence of the depth and power of God's love for you. He is sorting through the self of you to replace it with the glory and beauty of Jesus.

He was the one who began the work at the moment of your salvation. He sees the project's end in you although you right now can only dimly envision the beginning steps of this journey. Do you believe in the depth of your soul that He can complete the work He has begun? Some of that work will be completed here on earth, yet no matter how far you journey in pursuit of maturity in Christ, you will never fully reach its completeness while in the flesh. Praise God, the moment you see Jesus, you will be changed to be exactly as He is. Isn't it ironic that in God's economy, the key to moving deeper and closer to Jesus is complete dependency on Him alone and a firm resolution to not lean into your own understanding? How far will you lean into His understanding and His wisdom? (See Prov. 3:4–6.)

So you don't doubt His ability to complete the work. Do you doubt His willingness? How much do you trust the hand of the living one? In the depth and midst of your trial, doubt and confusion stand upon the Rock and resolutely proclaim, *"My God will deliver.* Yea, even if He slays me, I will trust in Him!"

In the pit of your soul, what image of God is immovable and unshakable? The extent to which you can cling to that immovable truth will determine to a large extent your response to God in the midst of trials, doubt, and uncertainty. Store those truths deep within your spirit now while there is time. Soak in His presence, and ponder His Word. Then the moment you need reinforcements, the lessons you have learned, the truths you have gained, and the Scripture you have hidden in your heart will arise to guide you to the place of a deep and firmly rooted trust in your Father.

Praise God, when you do not yet see the full story, when you do not yet understand, all you need to do is to cry out to Him and He will open your eyes more and more to the depth and majesty of His love and beauty. He will never leave you stagnant in your present comprehension and understanding if you call out to Him. He is waiting—patiently waiting—to hear your call!

> "Thus says the LORD who made the earth, the LORD who formed it to establish it, the LORD is His name, 'Call to Me and I will answer you, and I will tell you great and mighty things, which you do not know.' (Jer. 33:2–4)

# 27

# Follower's Fruit

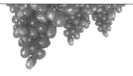

Now a Jew named Apollos, an Alexandrian by birth, an eloquent man, came to Ephesus; and he was mighty in the Scriptures. This man had been instructed in the way of the Lord; and being fervent in spirit, he was speaking and teaching accurately the things concerning Jesus, being acquainted only with the baptism of John; and he began to speak out boldly in the synagogue. But when Priscilla and Aquila heard him, they took him aside and explained to him the way of God more accurately. (Acts 18:24–26)

Dear Lord, teach me to speak with an instructed tongue! Teach me to worship with a pure heart! Oh, that I would sing more fully of the mercies of the Lord. Let complaining be put far away from me! May my eyes see the glory of the King, for I desire to speak of His majesty and wonder and might, but how can I speak of that which I do not know?

If I were to truly see Him,
I would not cease from exalting Him,
Throughout the night and into the day.
But if I were to see Him,
I wouldn't even be able to stand!
How great is His glory,
And unfathomable His ways!
Truly He is too high,
He is too grand for me.

How can I speak about,
That which I do not know?
Open my eyes, Lord, open my eyes!
Let me behold the glory of Your throne!
If I speak from my own wisdom,
I am but a fool,
For You are the only one,
Who knows innermost thoughts,
And intentions of a man.

You are the only one,
Who understands the depths of my
    heart.
How dare I speak before I have listened?
How dare I presume upon Your
    goodness?
Oh Father, have mercy!
How often do I lean into,
And depend on my own wisdom?
Lead me, guide me,
To stop and listen to You.

I must hearken unto Your voice,
For You are still speaking.
Your voice echoes throughout,
All generations since time began.
It shouts from the pages of Your book.
Its whispers like a gentle wind,
To the humble heart and contrite soul.
The broken one, oh Lord,
You will not despise.

The rocks cry with Your glory,
Creation groans to You,
To be liberated from sin's infestation.
Will Your people, Your chosen ones,
Pick up their banner of righteousness,
To offer the praise and adoration,
That is due to Your holy name?
The glory of the King surrounds us,
Do we see it?

Holy, holy, holy is Your name.

There are two parts to speaking with an instructed tongue:

- To live and speak what I hear from the throne room, whether
  it be by God's anointed teachers and worshippers, through the
  Scriptures, or by revelation from the Holy Spirit. It must be by
  God's time and place, not my own.

- To accept and live with what I do not understand, knowing that
  His hand undergirds it all.

What is the fruit from an instructed tongue? Is it to desire recognition?
Heed this warning and admonishment:

> *Better is **one** heart that has been unalterably changed by the Jesus
> in me than an abundance of smacking lips who only speak of life
> in Christ but do not live it.*

How do I access this life-changing power of God?

Some personal questions to ponder:

- Do I allow Jesus to flow through me to birth a thirst in others for His living water?

- Do I speak from my own understanding and try to lead others to model me? Forgive me, Lord!

- Do I earnestly seek to know the truth, knowing that the truth will indeed continually work to set me free? Am I freer today than I was yesterday?

- Do I follow the pattern of godliness I see in others? This is a start. Paul admonished us to follow his example.

- Do I go one step further and sit at the throne of grace and incline my ear and my heart to hear from the King? Jesus tells us His sheep know His voice and will not follow another. Am I listening?

- Who is following after me because of the Jesus in me?

- Do I count everything as loss in view of the glory of knowing Jesus better?

- Where is my focus—the glory of Jesus or the praise of man?

- What is the ultimate goal of my life? To avoid pain and seek comfort and consolation? Or to hear, "Well done faithful one, enter into your rest"? (See Matt. 25:21) Where will I rest, here or in heaven?

- Cease striving and know that "I am God," but at the same time keep pressing onward to the upward call of Jesus Christ. I can never give up either position. To truly be walking in the grace and power of God, these two things must coexist.

- Today is all I have. How will I spend it?

# 28

# He Is the Path

**He is the path**

> I am the way, the truth and the life; no one comes to the Father but through Me. (John 14:6)

**He is the path giver**

> "I know the plans I have for you," declares the Lord, "plans for your welfare and not calamity, to give you a future and a hope, then you will call upon Me and come and pray to Me, and I will listen to you. You will seek Me and find Me when you search for Me will all of your heart, I will be found by you," declares the Lord. (Jer. 29:11–14a)

**He is the path revealer**

> You will make known to me the path of life; in Your presence is fullness of joy; in Your right hand there are pleasures forever. (Ps. 16:11)

**He is the path illuminator**

> Your word is a lamp to my feet and a light to my path. (Ps. 119:105)

> Even the darkness is not dark to You, and the night is as bright as the day. Darkness and light are alike to You. (Ps. 139:12)

**He is the path protector**

> For He will give His angels charge concerning you, to guard you in all your ways. They will bear you up in their hands, that you do not strike your foot against a stone. (Ps. 91:11–12)

The LORD will protect you from all evil; He will keep your soul. The LORD will guard your going out and your coming in from this time forth and forever. (Ps. 121:7–8)

## He is the path director

No temptation has overtaken you but such as is common to man, and God is faithful, who will not allow you to be tempted beyond what you are able, but with the temptation will provide a way of escape also, so that you will be able to endure it. (1 Cor. 10:13)

## He is the path cleaner

If we say that we have no sin, we are deceiving ourselves and the truth is not in us. If we confess our sins, He is faithful and righteous to forgive us our sins and to cleanse us from all unrighteousness. (1 John 1:8–9)

## He is the path healer

For they disciplined us for a short time as seemed best to them, but He disciplines us for our good, so that we may share His holiness. All discipline for the moment seems not to be joyful, but sorrowful; yet to those who have been trained by it, afterwards it yields the peaceful fruit of righteousness. Therefore strengthen the hands that are weak and the knees that are feeble, and make straight paths for your feet, so that the limb which is lame may not be put out of joint, but rather be healed. Pursue peace with all men, and the sanctification without which no one will see the Lord. (Heb. 12:10–14)

## He is the path of peace

The steadfast of mind You will keep in perfect peace, because he trusts in You. (Isa. 26:3)

## He is the path sustainer

Cast your burden upon the LORD and He will sustain you; He will never allow the righteous to be shaken. (Ps. 55:22)

Now to Him who is able to keep you from stumbling, and to make you stand in the presence of His glory blameless with great joy, to the only God our Savior, through Jesus Christ our Lord, be glory, majesty, dominion and authority, before all time and now and forever. Amen. (Jude 1:24–25)

# 29

# Heart's Focus

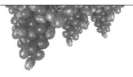

> Do not store up for yourselves treasures on earth, where moth and rust destroy, and where thieves break in and steal. But store up for yourselves treasures in heaven, where neither moth nor rust destroys, and where thieves do not break in or steal; for where your treasure is, there your heart will be also. (Matt. 6:19–21)

We were created to love and serve God, but in our instant gratification mindset, we have turned this totally around and often treat God as an errand boy whose job it is to serve us and meet our every need. True, He promises to give us the desires of our heart as we delight in Him, but somehow we focus on the receipt of our hearts' desires rather than delighting in Him. We have gotten this all backward. He tells us to "Seek ye first the kingdom of God" and then all these things will be added to you. (See Matt. 6:33.)

When did our eyes shift off of the kingdom and onto this earth? When did the crux of our prayers begin to revolve around, "Give me this, I need that," instead of dwelling on the majesty of our King? Truly if we will sit at His feet and gaze into His face, the needs of this earth will begin to fade away as we behold the glorious King. We so desperately need to seclude ourselves for a while with the lover of our souls. Choose to draw aside with Him and do nothing more than love on Him, rejoice and praise Him, and *listen*. When this becomes a priority, we will find that He eagerly bends down low to meet us in that place and fill our hearts with unspeakable joy and peace. He gladly equips us with the wisdom, direction, and energy to face whatever is assailing us in the earthly realm.

Our level of worry is inversely proportional to the quality of time we have spent at the Savior's feet. We can't expect to be released from anxiety's grasp with a thoughtless prayer of, "God bless me, amen." It all deals with the position of our thoughts and expectations as we draw into His presence. Is our primary motive to be blessed by God or to be a blessing to Him? We need refocus time daily to release us from the pull of self-centered thoughts and the lusts of self-promotion. Actually, we need it every moment as we encounter the twists and turns of life.

When leaving the holy place with God, do not let go of His hand. He will continue to hold His own. He will never let His child go. Our awareness of His nearness and the tenderness of His love are dependent on how eagerly we reach up to Him to seek after Him. He is calling each of our names. Can you hear Him? He deeply desires to share the depths of His heart. He already knows the darkest secrets that we have vainly tried to seal off from notice. Will we open up to Him? All clean and pure desire is birthed in the heart of God. If we will listen closely to Him, He will begin to share His passions with us, and we will begin to see those about us, and the world as a whole, with new eyes. Our confidence level will increase because it has shifted from us and our meager resources into the hands of a mighty and powerful God.

# 30

# Voice of the Lord

> God, after He spoke long ago to the fathers in the prophets in many portions and in many ways, in these last days has spoken to us in His Son, whom He appointed heir of all things, through whom also He made the world. And He is the radiance of His glory and the exact representation of His nature, and upholds all things by the word of His power. When He had made purification of sins, He sat down at the right hand of the Majesty on high, having become as much better than the angels, as He has inherited a more excellent name than they. (Heb. 1:1–4)

> But the word of God came unto Shemaiah the man of God, saying, Speak unto Rehoboam, the son of Solomon, king of Judah, and unto all the house of Judah and Benjamin, and to the remnant of the people, saying, *Thus saith the LORD,* Ye shall not go up, nor fight against your brethren the children of Israel: return every man to his house; for this thing is from me. They hearkened therefore to the word of the LORD, and returned to depart, according to the word of the LORD. (1 Kings 12:22–24, emphasis added)

"Thus saith the Lord"—this is the voice of a prophet! Notice how a timely word from God avoided needless strife and slaughter.

This is our inheritance in Christ—to walk in the revelation and spoken word of God. Are we speaking His Word, the words that have been written and passed down through the generations? There is incredible power in the Word of God—use it! This is an everlasting word, spoken by the prophets and apostles and recorded for our benefit. Stand on it, pray through it, and declare it. God speaks through His Word. We all would say, "Hallelujah and amen" to this. But have you considered that God is still speaking today? He is speaking to those who have ears to hear. Are we hearing His voice? Are we even listening for it? If we hear it, are we declaring His present-day word that He reveals through His prophets? Will we go boldly forth, proclaiming the goodness and glory of our King? Walk in faith to trample the voice of fear!

God created the earth in six days. God spoke and it was. God's prophets must clearly listen and boldly speak out that which God is prompting them to speak. God works through the spoken word. This is how He birthed creation. Why do we believe that He would stop using His voice through the voice of His people? He has positioned some to be His voice crying in the wilderness, "Behold, the Lamb of God" and "thus saith the Lord"! There is a timely word for the right moment, and the time and the word are birthed in the heart of God.

Am I, are you, in a position to hear and follow, to listen and obey? Will we watch with expectant hearts and speak with boldness when God leads us forward? This is the mark of a humble heart and a bondservant of Jesus. He is calling us into a new day saturated with a purer revelation of the depth and power of His love toward those who believe. Doing His will is the bread we feed on, the strength we lean on, and the *joy* of our hearts. As we walk forward with a joy that cannot be quenched (because it does not depend on anything temporal), a radiant voice of praise and glory will spring forth from among God's people. We are all being called to walk in the fullness of Jesus Christ, called to proclaim His excellence, exalt His name, and carry forth His banner of praise.

We must be bold and courageous to walk into new waters holding onto the hand of Jesus, knowing He will not steer us wrong or let us go. Are your feet still touching the ground of familiarity? Don't you hunger and thirst for a new move of God, for the joy of the Lord to break forth on the day of a new dawn? Behold weeping is for the night, but new joy comes in the morning. (See Ps. 30:4–5.) Rejoice in your King. Proclaim that which He is laying on your heart. Be bold and courageous. Speak it out. Sing it out: *the Lord is indeed my Shepherd, and I shall not want!* (See Ps. 23:1)

Remember, one day everyone will pay homage to Jesus Christ, for He is forever Lord. For now we are His feet and hands, but if we will listen and follow His directions, we can also be His voice to this generation. We need to be aligned so closely and intimately with God that we will speak His heart unto the people. It is the day for a new word, a new power, and a new manifestation to reign down from on high. He is waiting for the faith to birth it, for the prayers to release it, and for a desperate dependency upon Him covered in love that is so strong, so full that it will abandon all else to follow the voice of the Beloved. Love will deliver it to the right place that has been prepared beforehand by the hand of God. He will use and exalt the humble. His power will flow through them like powerful running mountain streams, but the proud will stumble and fall at the hand of the Lord. He alone is our shield and our defense, so go forward into the battle with joyful singing. Let the praise and the glory of God be both your front and rear guard. Boldly proclaim all that He shows and reveals to you. Let your voice be totally His. You are His; He will not misguide you or lead you astray. He is the wind under your wings. He is your shield and shelter. He will equip you, fortify you, test you, refine you, and empower you. He will never let you go! Go forward in the joy and admonition of the Lord.

# 31

# God's Revelation Word

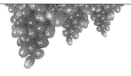

> So will My Word be which goes forth from My Mouth; It will not return to Me empty, without accomplishing what I desire and without succeeding in the matter for which I sent it. (Isa. 55:11)

God's revelation includes not only Scripture but also the Word of God that is being spoken through the Holy Spirit, a Word that is spoken for this particular day. Feed on today's manna written in the Word of God, but also trust in a God whose Word is living and active and sharper than a two-edged sword. He is still speaking to His people promises for today, both from Scripture and directly into our hearts. Listen, trust Him, and in faith, proclaim what He is giving to you today. Be sure to ask for discernment whether this is for you personally or to be shared with others.

Remember His present-day word for today will never contradict Scripture. However, it may stretch our understanding of it. It may very well propel us beyond a surface understanding of the Word and open up to us the deeper heart of God. I fear that this is where many Christians stumble. A new word of God is given, and although it does line up with Scripture, it does not fit our preconceived interpretation of the Word. In ignorance we reject it and miss the beauty and glory of God that He wishes to bless us with in that moment. Are we willing to walk into the unexpected and untried if God is leading us there? Will we miss the present move of God because we are so wrapped up in the way we do things? Do we love God, or do we love our conception of God?

> Oh Lord, forgive me for my low expectations and my willingness to walk in the sameness of yesterday. Give me a

passion for Your new work today. Help me to feed on today's manna, for yesterday's was for the day gone by, and if used for today, I will find it moldy and useless. Help me to truly walk in new life in You!

Scripture is the road under our feet that keeps us on the right path. Revelation words and works are given for the need of the moment, just like changes in speed limit signs. These present-day words and works tell us to slow down here and don't rush God's timing, or *now* is the time, pay attention (i.e., speed up) so you don't miss the current outpouring and work of God.

Both our immersion in the Word and our willingness to accept a new word from God must work in unison to render us useful in the kingdom's work. If God were to translate you to a different place, like Philip in Acts 8:26–36, would you squander that time worrying about what had happened, or would you go forth in trust and joy, proclaiming the goodness of God? Will we trust God enough to accept and welcome His present-day moving? Will we be wise and discerning enough to tell the difference between our Father's voice and that of the enemy? Remember, the sheep know the Shepherd's voice and will follow no other. (See John 10:1–5.) Trust in God to speak to your heart in way that you can recognize and understand. Follow Him into the newness of today, and do not reject a move of His hand if it looks different from what you saw yesterday.

Come, Lord Jesus, speak to my hungry heart today!

When we approach the Word with only an academic mindset, we will come away feeling dull, dry, void of power, and useless to achieve world impact. When we meet with the living God inside the pages of His text, the words almost leap off the page with a fiery intensity and the power of purification. The Spirit-filled and -breathed Word of God brings new life, high devotion, fire for God, and an outpouring of love that would be totally impossible with our own resources. Where do we want to be? We will not enter into a fuller manifestation of the glory of God unless we allow the Word to fully penetrate our hearts, souls, and minds. It has to impact the whole man, and here is where we as the American church fall; we think that by giving only mental agreement to the Word that we are living in the fullness of God. Our faith must have feet! But those faith-filled feet won't take us anywhere until the Word permeates every part of our being!

Come, Lord Jesus, come and so fill Your people with the fullness of who You are that we will absolutely burst if we do not share the glorious news of Jesus! This is the true life of Jesus followers, being so rapturously in love with their Lord that they can never get enough. In turn they can never give enough of the Lord's love away.

Oh Lord, please renew my heart, my passions, and my every thought that all things in me would worship and long after You in ways I have never known before!

Come, Jesus, come—satisfy my thirst for You, yet cause it to burn brighter and deeper at the same time. My longing for You absolutely hurts. Come feed Your sheep. Come, Jesus, come!

# 32

# Forceful Praise

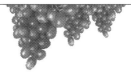

From the days of John the Baptist until now the kingdom of heaven suffers violence, and violent men take it by force. (Matt 11:12)

The Law and the Prophets were proclaimed until John; since that time the gospel of the kingdom of God has been preached, and everyone is forcing his way into it. (Luke 16:16)

- Do you want to take hold of the kingdom of God right here and right now?

- Do you want to live in the glory of heaven here on this fallen earth?

- What are you hungry for—the praise of men or the pleasure of your Master?

- Will you willingly offer Him a sacrifice of praise?

Sacrificial praise costs us something. There is an agony of spirit, a desperate hunger for more of God that births it. Sacrificial praise is worship with voice, heart, mind, body, and spirit that is rooted in God's character alone, independent of our situation and circumstances. This is the truest form of praise, and it is the first step into *forceful praise* that ushers in the glory of God and His kingdom. It paves the way to unleash a new move, a fresh outpouring of the mercies and love of God!

Do I want to engage in forceful praise? Do I really want to see the kingdom of heaven invade this old, weary land? Am I passionate for a deeper wonder of who God is?

*Aggressive praise* is a weapon. Few have just begun to take hold of the hilt of this sword! We retreat too often into the feel-good praise and run to praise as our shelter and shield. This is a baby step, and we must move beyond it if we want to usher in the glory of God. Sheltering praise that extols God as our Rock, Shelter, and Shield will always be there to undergird, support, and strengthen us as we advance into the fray of the battle between righteousness and unrighteousness. Will we also advance with praise, declaring the power and glory of God, which can shine into any situation to pierce the darkness and draw men's souls back to Him? This is the praise that leaps over the wall into the enemy's camp to release the captives! For their sake, we must advance in the praise realm and not fall back!

Give glory to God in all things! The more we grab hold of the intensity of God's glory, the sharper and purer our praise will become, and we will come to understand that glorious God-centered praise is an extraordinarily powerful weapon.

Stand and listen, hear and be changed! The drumbeat of heaven is growing louder and more intense. Do we hear it? Do not doubt or fear. God will lead His own further and closer into His heart and His passions. Lean hard into Him; seek Him while He still can be found! Draw near to God. Ask to hear His heartbeat, and be willing to share in His joys and His pain and sorrow over the sins of this earth. Advance, saints, grab hold of God, and move forward! Let the majesty of His name be our front and rear guard and thereby proclaim the victory of the cross every moment of our day!

Go forward with boldness. Let God's courage in you shine. Keep your feet on the narrow path! Do not let doubt and fear toss you about. Remember, you belong to God, and He has you covered and will see you safely home; but how many others will follow your footsteps? The fuller your praise, the more God's grace will flow down thicker and denser, and the deeper your impact will be upon all those around you. As you walk the narrow road of faith, remember if God is for you, who can be against you?

Trust in God's ability to bring forth what He has promised. Trust Him, praise Him, and watch for His deliverance. Don't settle for anything less than the pleasure of your Lord. Wait for the fullness of all God has stored up and planned for you since the foundation of time. Keep pressing in with an attitude of praise and adoration for your King! As you wait, God is building your character and pruning your attitudes to put you in the right place when the blessings begin to fall. If they were given too early, you would hoard them and idolize them. By waiting, God's character is tested and revealed in you. As you wait, God will be found to be trustworthy. The deeper your trust in Him, the more grace He will give you to wait. The more you wait in the stillness of spirit, the more the glory of God shines through you!

- What do you agonize over?

- Do you seek after relief and release from circumstances?

- Do you hunger for blessings to flow from His hand?

- Are you more zealous for His reputation than your own?

- Will you let God make you hungry for more of Him?

- Are you hungry enough for God to cry, "Lord show me more of You or I will perish!"

- Is He truly your fountain of refreshment, your foundation of praise?

Saints, let us join hearts and hands and enter into the presence of God with a reverence so deep and wonder so bright that it will be our joy, the very essence of our spirits to follow where He leads. Truly once we have really tasted of the waters of life, we are ruined for anything else. Will we hunger for the praise of heaven to pour down upon the earth? Or will we continue in the paths of yesterday and only engage in the praise of earth reaching up to heaven? We need *both* to engage in forceful, aggressive praise that ushers in the kingdom of God.

Come, Lord Jesus, feed our hungry hearts and let us thirst ever more for an increased revelation of the intenseness of Your glory!

# 33

# Groaning

> But if we hope for what we do not see, with perseverance we
> wait eagerly for it. In the same way the Spirit also helps our
> weakness; for we do not know how to pray as we should, but
> the Spirit Himself intercedes for us with groanings too deep
> for words; and He who searches the hearts knows what the
> mind of the Spirit is, because He intercedes for the saints
> according to the will of God. (Rom. 8:25–27)

What an assurance that as I pray, God's will is done and God's heart is revealed to me and in me. The Spirit takes my earth-bound prayers and fits and shapes them for the kingdom of heaven! All He really asks of me is a willingness to lift my hands and my heart toward heaven. He listens intently to the groaning of my spirit even when I am not consciously aware of the burden that may be lodged deep in my heart. Even then the Spirit is lifting the agony of my heart's desire before the throne of grace. Before He presents it to the Father, He washes out the self-serving attitudes and self-inflated desires and seeks for the morsel of truth that will glorify God, edify and heal the saints, and reach the lost. Those are the groaning so deep, so integral to the Father's heart that the Spirit stands in my stead and pleads my case before the throne in the language of heaven—groans of longing and pain too deep and too profound for words. Again, it all depends upon God. He searches my heart. He brings my prayer into the throne room. He hears and understands the full ramification of the prayer's request and ripples that will result from its fulfillment. He sees throughout the generations and knows how the answer to what seems to me to be one simple prayer will impact and change generations to come. No wonder the Spirit groans with the holy weight of it all!

The weight of it all is unimaginable. God knows what I long to pursue in prayer even before the thought has entered my conscious mind. Even before I conceive of a need, He knows it. He hears the prayer that will be birthed because of that need. He is ready to carry it before the throne the moment my spirit spits out the request in the depth of my heart. It may not even reach the awareness of my mind. The Spirit searches all of me: my mind, my heart, and my emotions. He weaves these all together and takes their intent and passions and presents them before the throne in a form suitable to be presented to the King of Kings and Lord of all creation.

Beyond this, God holds all the prayers I have ever prayed—even those uttered long ago and forgotten. He combines the prayers offered days ago, the prayers I am currently laboring over, and the prayers I have yet to pray. He sees all of them, in their individuality and in their cohesion, and knows how they will nestle together to draw me into a greater state of holiness and unity with the heart of the Father. It is mind boggling to think that God holds my prayers from the infancy of my Christian walk and weaves them together with today's trials and tomorrow's dreams. He sees them all concurrently, and He knows what prayers He needs to prompt me to pray to orient my heart toward His kingdom's work. The extent of His knowledge over my prayer life is indeed humbling. But when I take a step back and think that He holds the prayers of *all* His children in the same fashion, I can only shake my head in awe and ponder. How mighty is my God, and how incredible is the depth and purity of His love for His own!

> But just as it is written, "THINGS WHICH EYE HAS NOT SEEN AND EAR HAS NOT HEARD, AND which HAVE NOT ENTERED THE HEART OF MAN, ALL THAT GOD HAS PREPARED FOR THOSE WHO LOVE HIM." For to us God revealed them through the Spirit; for the Spirit searches all things, even the depths of God. (1 Cor. 2:9–10)

# 34

# Freedom in Nothingness

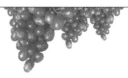

He who has the bride is the bridegroom; but the friend of the bridegroom, who stands and hears him, rejoices greatly because of the bridegroom's voice. So this joy of mine has been made full. He must increase, but I must decrease. He who comes from above is above all, he who is of the earth is from the earth and speaks of the earth. He who comes from heaven is above all. (John 3:29–31)

I have nothing to prove
I am but dust
I am only a speck in the continuum of time
I am only a whisper in the midst of a
Magnificent orchestra
Nothing is to my credit
All that is me, all that I do
Goes only to the glory of God.

So who am I zealous for?
Is it for my reputation?
Heaven forbid
Is it for my comfort, convenience?
Lord, help me!
Is it to leave a legacy?
What and in whom do I trust?

Any legacy left in myself and my abilities
Will soon rot away
The only hope
The only lasting power
The only thing worthy
Of my attention and focus
Of my heart's passion
Is the glory of God!

Everything done for His name
Everything thought, felt, and experienced
Is only worthy to the point
That it drew me closer to Jesus
Do I reflect Him in all I do?
What is my heart's motive?
Is it to draw attention to myself?

Or is it to lead others
Into a deeper
And purer love of Jesus Christ?
That is the only legacy
With lasting power
The only legacy with eternal impact
The only one worthy of Jesus' name
The only one that will last.

So who will I follow?
The shifting winds of this society
With nothing firm on which to
    anchor their hope?
Do I move because it feels good?
Do I act to satisfy my physical cravings?
Do I seek approval and justification of
    my actions?
Or because it would please my Lord?

In whom do I place my trust?
Am I zealous for His reputation?
Or mine?
Jesus, search my heart
Let me know You
As I have been known
Lead me to glorify You
In word, thought, and deed.

I must become less
So You can become more
Move me out of the way
And let my every thought glorify You
So You will shine through me.
Radiate through my nothingness
'Til all the world sees is Jesus!

# 35

# Heart of Hope

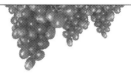

And hope does not disappoint, because the love of God has been poured out within our hearts through the Holy Spirit who was given to us. For while we were still helpless, at the right time Christ died for the ungodly. (Rom. 5:5–6)

But for You

There would be no hope
There would be no peace
There would be no goodwill
There would be no forgiveness
There would be no healing
There would be no mercy
There would be no grace
There would be no righteousness
And holiness would be a joke
There would be no eternal hope
The grave would boast its victory
Strength would wither
And man's plans would go astray
Evil would reign
And terror would rule
But for God

Yet the Almighty Rules!

He sifts the king's heart like water
And raises and removes kingdoms
He laughs at the plans of evil men
And uses them for His purposes
He abases the proud heart
But gives grace to the humble
He bends down to extend mercy
And gives it freely to all who ask
He listens to His children's cry
And He comforts their distress
He rejoices when we praise Him
And He bears our sorrow in love
He gives knowledge and wisdom
To those who faithfully ask
He works in all our tribulations
And shows us His powerful name
He lifts us above our circumstance
And gives a hope that will not die
His forgiveness has no limits
And He extends His graceful love

He crowns us with heaven's glory
And He calls us His very own
His counsel stands forever
And His kingdom will never end

But Christ was faithful as a Son over His house—whose house we are, if we hold fast our confidence and the boast of our hope firm until the end. (Heb. 3:6)

# 36

# Irresistible Summons

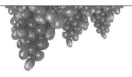

> So it came about on the third day, when it was morning, that there were thunder and lightning flashes and a thick cloud upon the mountain and a very loud trumpet sound, so that all the people who were in the camp trembled. And Moses brought the people out of the camp to meet God, and they stood at the foot of the mountain. Now Mount Sinai was all in smoke because the LORD descended upon it in fire; and its smoke ascended like the smoke of a furnace, and the whole mountain quaked violently. When the sound of the trumpet grew louder and louder, Moses spoke and God answered him with thunder. The LORD came down on Mount Sinai, to the top of the mountain; and the LORD called Moses to the top of the mountain, and Moses went up. (Ex. 19:16–20)

Imagine the scene at Mount Sinai. Thick smoke, fire, and a violent trembling covered the mountain. To the natural eye, it would appear that the mountain was erupting as the smoke ascended from its peaks and fire covered its heights. As if that weren't enough, the mountain also began to shake with the tremors of an earthquake, and the sound of a trumpet's blast filled the air. The visual impact would have been enough to cause anyone to shake in his or her sandals. I suppose I would have not only been shaking but would have been looking for the nearest scrub bush to hide behind!

As the Creator descended, the surface of the earth could not bear up under His incredible glory. It had to shake under the weight of God's presence. Heaven touched earth. A trumpet from the courtyards of heaven announced the wonder of God visiting His people. The piercing blast summoned the people to bow and reverence almighty God. There would be no denying or rationalizing away these occurrences. Surely Jehovah was in the midst of His people. Trembling seems like an understatement. Fear must have been as thick as a dense fog. These people were witnessing the glory of God descending upon the mountain. Who would even dare to approach? The mountain appeared to be unstable at best with its quaking, fire, and flame. Venturing toward its heights would draw only the heartiest spirit or one steeped in the height of arrogance. Moses was neither of these. He was called. He was called by God Himself.

Prior to Moses' ascent toward this holy mount, he spoke with God. During this interchange, the trumpet's volume increased dramatically, almost as a heavenly exclamation point to mark the eternal significance of this moment. Moses spoke. Surely the trumpet's volume covered his words so that his communication with God was veiled from the people. Yet no one could deny God's answer as He thundered in reply. Finally the stage was set. God was prepared to meet His people in the power, strength, and might of the eternal King. The significance of this moment could not be missed or forgotten. It marked the moment when the Eternal One bowed down to earth to impart a code of holiness to guide and protect His people during their sojourning days on earth. Moses was chosen, and Moses was called. He was called to draw close to God and to receive from His hand the instructions for the people God loved. How could he deny this summons?

We can hardly imagine the raw power and glory of this moment. No one has seen God and lived, yet Moses was being called up into His presence. God had prepared Moses for this encounter years earlier when He captured Moses' attention through the burning bush. It was in this encounter that God met Moses in his fear and addressed Moses' insecurities. The bush's fire cleansed away the reticence and seeds of denial that would have impeded Moses' response to God's summons at the foot of Mount Sinai. Moses was all in. He was chosen and covered by God. He had learned to converse with God, and he had learned obedience through the trials of affliction. There was no turning back. He was God's instrument, and if that meant ascending a burning, quaking mountain, there was no other choice but to start climbing. God called, and Moses answered.

God is still calling today. He is looking for those who will follow with their whole hearts. He calls and seeks for those who will lay aside their own passions so He can cover them with the cloak of His holy mission to bring His glory down to earth. The amazing thing is that as we respond to God's summons, He gently tweaks our hearts' affections and realigns them to march in cadence with the heartbeat of heaven. He has given us everything we need for godliness and holiness. All He asks of us is a willing heart to step out and receive all He wants to pour into us. Stop, look, and listen. The Lord is calling. As long as we have breath, it is never too late to respond to His summons. What is your personal burning bush moment? It is only the beginning of a glorious and exciting journey with the Lord of heaven and King of our hearts.

> Moses said to the people, "Do not be afraid; for God has come in order to test you, and in order that the fear of Him may remain with you, so that you may not sin." (Ex. 20:20)

# 37

# Faith's Test

> Finally then, brethren, we request and exhort you in the Lord Jesus, that as you received from us instruction as to how you ought to walk and please God (just as you actually do walk), *that you excel still more.* (1 Thess. 4:1, emphasis added)

> Then Amalek came and fought against Israel at Rephidim. So Moses said to Joshua, "Choose men for us and go out, fight against Amalek. *Tomorrow* I will station myself on the top of the hill with the staff of God in my hand." Joshua did as Moses told him, and fought against Amalek; and Moses, Aaron, and Hur went up to the top of the hill. (Ex. 17:8–10, emphasis added)

God's ways are higher than our ways. Our mindset is often geared toward the quick fix, the ready answer, the instant solution. Very few relish and welcome the opportunity to dwell in the waiting room called patience. Yet it is in those times of waiting that God tries us and tests us. Oh, He already knows what is in our hearts so much better than we do. Our hearts are deceptive and inherently wicked, and we desperately need God's pruning and sorting to clarify our thought processes and purify our hearts.

Our Lord gives us instruction for our welfare and benefit. Our level of obedience speaks volumes as to who is really on the throne in our hearts. Will we lean on our own understanding or willingly place our hands in the hands of our Father with the trust level of a small child? No wonder Jesus tells us that we must enter the kingdom with the hearts of children. Their level of intimate faith places full confidence in the object of their trust. We must do the same and place all of our hopes, dreams, and aspirations in the hands of the one who made us. He is the dream giver, so wouldn't He also be the dream fulfiller? Who else is more trustworthy than God?

Joshua was faced with a formidable enemy. They appeared as giants to the nation of Israel, and so Joshua sought the leadership and advice of Moses. He was told to go and fight and that Moses would intercede for him "tomorrow." Why would Moses delay? Why would Joshua be led to fight without his leader's prayer covering for a day? It appears that Joshua may have spent that first day ordering the troops and preparing for battle, and when the moment of crucial conflict began, Moses would be in place to cover the nation with his rod upheld and the glory of God would cover His people. But not on the first day; Moses would intercede only in the thick of battle.

Joshua was a mighty man of courage, and in this moment of conflict and decision, his dedication to Moses, and thus to God, was tested. He accepted Moses' council and went about his duty to order and prepare the men of Israel to fight. He did not argue with Moses and insist that he enter into the presence of God immediately on his behalf. He accepted Moses' counsel and went about his duty, trusting in God to deliver them through Moses, tomorrow.

In our hurry-up world, we cannot rush God. His timing is perfect. He knows that in the time of our waiting, our trust level will be tested and stretched. He knows what we each need and when and how we need it. He knows when to send out our heavenly Moses with rod outstretched to bring down the provision and glory of God into our lives. At times the waiting may seem like an eternity, but remember, beloved, with God one day is as a thousand years and a thousand years as a day. As you wait, remember that God has your back, and He has already sent out His heavenly army to go before you to prepare your way. You just can't see it yet.

Bring your heart's cry to Him. Let Him seek out the depth of your heart. Then wait for His intervention with a rekindled hope. Move forward with a strong expectation for His intervention and direct your feet toward utter and complete obedience while you wait for your delivery. Step out in faith where He is calling you to walk. Remember as you submit all things to Him, He will keep you from falling and catching your foot in the enemy's nets. With this perspective, the waiting room will begin to lose its sting as God moves on your heart to understand that the waiting just prepares you to receive more of His presence and a deeper level of purification and fortification of your level of trust. It strengthens you to excel even more in your walk of faith. This all starts with that first step to move out where God has called while trusting in Him to meet every need as you follow His direction.

# 38

# Mark of Sonship

> For this is a rebellious people, false sons, sons who refuse to listen to the instruction of the Lord. Who say to the seers, "You must not see visions," and to the prophets, "You must not prophesy to us what is right. Speak to us pleasant words. Prophesy illusions. Get out of the way, turn aside from the path. Let us hear no more about the Holy One of Israel." (Isa. 30:9–11)

With sonship there comes a great deal of responsibility. We are called to a higher standard and are measured against the very holiness of God Himself. He calls us to follow. We are to walk after His lead even when we do not understand or even particularly like where He is telling us to go. There will be many voices vying for our attention, and temptation will swirl about our feet like nipping dogs. But God calls us to lay all of these things aside and cling to that which is good, pure, holy, righteous, and just. He calls us to lean in close and to listen to His heartbeat.

Yet before we can even try to do this, we must divorce ourselves from our affection for approval from those about us. We must truly walk in this world and not be of it. This seems like an impossible task since we are surrounded by culture and influenced so deeply by the media. Their message seeps into our spirits swiftly and often unannounced or unnoticed by us. When we become settled into our routines and comfortable with our state of spiritual progress, it becomes easy to subtly move off the track of the pursuit of holiness.

We tend to ruminate with what we presently know and base our current decisions solely on the lessons learned from prior experiences. We stop hungering and thirsting for more of God's righteousness. When this complacency descends, we quickly become mired in our present state of revelation. Our spirits begin to languish as we put our feet up in rest. When a deep hunger for God begins to diminish and we are willing to abide in our present state of spiritual enlightenment, we are truly feeding on yesterday's manna. Oh, it tastes good and is deeply pleasant to our senses, but if we linger here too long, we will begin to think that we have arrived and that we need only tread the waters of our current state of godliness and work and wait for the glory of God to bring us home.

Yet God desires to draw us deeper into His heart of love and revelation. Part of walking with Him in the secret place of our affections is to share with Him the sorrows and burdens of His heart. It will not be all wine and roses. Jesus was called a man of sorrows. As His followers, are we not also called to share in what burdens His heart? How often do we weep and lament over the corrupt spiritual condition of our nation? How often do we raise our heads above our own personal concerns to engage in a battle for the heart and soul of an entire people? Yes, salvation is rendered one spirit at a time, but do we burn to see a mighty revival descend and sweep hundreds, thousands into the kingdom of God? Will our complacency cost someone else a chance to abide in eternity with God? Will we join with God's heart and plead for His mercy to descend upon our nation?

Our biggest threat is not stumbling into some deeply offensive and obnoxious sin. It is settling into what we already know and have already experienced. This is such a subtle pitfall because it sneaks in under our radar. This attitude extinguishes a desire to lean harder into God to perceive and glean a deeper comprehension of who He is and how incredibly profound is His holiness. When the hunger we once knew as new believers starts to subside, we are in peril of hunkering down, fellowshipping with the saints, and becoming stinky and immovable as stagnant water.

Water, to be kept clean and pure, must keep on moving, flowing, and trickling down the riverbed. So too we must continue on looking, listening, and yearning for a deeper revelation and understanding of the depth and purity of our King. True, there will be rocks and boulders along the river's course. When we meet those obstacles, there will be turbulence and upset. But when we fully trust in the one who can deliver us from death, we will find that at the other end of the rapids there is a tranquil pool full of refreshing water that will plunge the depths of God to an extent that we can only now vaguely dream about. This spiritual "shooting of the rapids" begins when we willingly, once again, bring ourselves before our Creator, lay aside our own agenda, and plead to hear the direction of His heartbeat. Are you willing to take up your paddle and jump in the raft with Him?

> Therefore the Lord longs to be gracious to you, and therefore
> He waits on high to have compassion on you. For the Lord is
> a God of justice; how blessed are all those who long for Him.
> (Isa. 30:18)

# 39

# Humility's Perspective

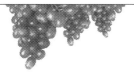

> You adulteresses, do you not know that friendship with the world is hostility toward God? Therefore whoever wishes to be a friend of the world makes himself an enemy of God. Or do you think that the Scripture speaks to no purpose: "He jealously desires the Spirit which He has made to dwell in us"? But He gives a greater grace. Therefore it says, "GOD IS OPPOSED TO THE PROUD, BUT GIVES GRACE TO THE HUMBLE." (James 4:4–6)

> Humble yourselves in the presence of the Lord, and He will exalt you. Do not speak against one another, brethren. He who speaks against a brother or judges his brother, speaks against the law and judges the law; but if you judge the law, you are not a doer of the law but a judge of it. (James 4:10–11)

Humility—the one word in our Christian vocabulary that can bring all of us to our knees in abject confession and hopeless confusion. It is often said that the moment one confesses a spirit of humility, one has just lost it! How do we pursue such an elusive goal? Honesty leads us to admit that as we seek this attribute, it flows through our hands like quicksilver. It appears to be unobtainable and just beyond our reach. When we are blatantly honest, it appears that this precious, godly spirit is one that we truly cannot claim until we see Jesus face to face. How do we pursue a heart of humility?

In pondering this, God posed this thought: "Is this even the right question to ask?" The framework of this question subtly reveals the position of the heart; sadly, a self-focus! Should humility be the object of our pursuit, or in seeking after it, has the enemy again diverted our attention from what is truly important? Unknowingly, in trying to emulate a godly attitude, we can swiftly be drawn back into the battle of self-interest versus God's glory!

True humility comes when our confidence rests completely on the one who loves us, saved us, and indwells us rather than in our own innate abilities and talents. It is the difference between, "Yeah, I did that" and "Wow, look at what God has done!" The truly humble one, in his heart of hearts, will not cling to any compliment but rather lay them all at the feet of Jesus in an act of selfless worship. In this moment, his worship and adoration of God grows exponentially, and he finds that there is no greater joy than rejoicing in the abundance and majesty of God almighty. Focusing on humility just draws us further away from it; our focus, of necessity, must be on God alone. It is He who has prepared our good works beforehand, so why do we think we can take credit for them? It is He who puts all of the pieces and players into place to accomplish a particular work. It is He who has gifted us to serve. It is He who births the passion in our spirit for a particular act of service or worship. So why do we garner the praise unto ourselves?

The truly humble will not be able to recognize this attribute in their spirits. Their focus is rooted and centered in God alone. Any success, any failure, is just a prompt to bring all things to the feet of Jesus! The deeper our love for God and the purer our hearts, the sweeter our humility of spirit will become. The beauty of all this is that as we grow deeper in love with our Lord, our hearts and affections will begin to line up more and more with Him, until our reputation is of no account and all that matters is that the glory of Jesus is radiating through His people to the dark and hungry places of this earth.

Humility is largely exhibited through our interactions with others. Do we truly consider them before ourselves? God encourages us to bear one another's burdens and so fulfill the law of Christ. We need to lay down our agendas and reach out to the hurting and suffering and within the same breath, be able to deeply rejoice with those who are rejoicing. This seems like a tall order, until we remember once again that we can do all things through Christ who gives us strength. (See Phil. 4:13.)

So look up and rejoice in the God of your salvation. Let His love and mercy flow through you to meet the needs of those who are hurting. Give thanks as His abundant grace moves through you to bring the loving touch of Jesus down to earth. As you begin to move the complete focus of your praise heavenward, the blossom of humility will begin to open and shed its sweet fragrance all around you. People will then begin to see Jesus walking among us, and we will all be changed!

> Is anyone among you suffering? Then he must pray. Is anyone cheerful? He is to sing praises. Is anyone among you sick? Then he must call for the elders of the church and they are to pray over him, anointing him with oil in the name of the Lord; and the prayer offered in faith will restore the one who is sick, and the Lord will raise him up, and if he has committed sins, they will be forgiven him. Therefore, confess your sins to one another, and pray for one another so that you may be healed. The effective prayer of a righteous man can accomplish much. (James 5:13–16)

> But whatever things were gain to me, those things I have counted as loss for the sake of Christ. More than that, I count all things to be loss in view of the surpassing value of knowing Christ Jesus my Lord, for whom I have suffered the loss of all things, and count them but rubbish so that I may gain Christ, and may be found in Him, not having a righteousness of my own derived from the Law, but that which is through faith in Christ, the righteousness which comes from God on the basis of faith, that I may know Him and the power of His resurrection and the fellowship of His sufferings, being conformed to His death; in order that I may attain to the resurrection from the dead. (Phil. 3:7–11)

# 40

# Cloak of God

But seeing the wind, he became frightened, and beginning to sink, he cried out, "Lord, save me!" Immediately Jesus stretched out His hand and took hold of him, and said to him, "You of little faith, why did you doubt?" When they got into the boat, the wind stopped. And those who were in the boat worshiped Him, saying, "You are certainly God's Son!" When they had crossed over, they came to land at Gennesaret. And when the men of that place recognized Him, they sent word into all that surrounding district and brought to Him all who were sick; and they implored Him that they might just touch the fringe of His cloak; and as many as touched it were cured. (Matt. 14:30–36)

When Boaz had eaten and drunk and his heart was merry, he went to lie down at the end of the heap of grain; and she came secretly, and uncovered his feet and lay down. It happened in the middle of the night that the man was startled and bent forward; and behold, a woman was lying at his feet. He said, "Who are you?" And she answered, "I am Ruth your maid. So spread your covering over your maid, for you are a close relative." (Ruth 3:7–9)

If only the fringe of Jesus' cloak heals, imagine what is ours when He throws His covering over us to envelop us completely. It is enough to leave one breathless with wonder! All that He is, is ours! Why, as His people, do we not appropriate this? Why do we cower in fear and ineffectiveness? Why are we not bringing down the fortresses of evil that lurk everywhere? Instead we settle for living in this land of misty shadows when we should at all times be walking in the full manifestation of the glory of God!

He threw His cloak over His children at the cross. Christ's blood covers all of our sin. We must stop clinging to the old manner of life and walk in the fullness of the anointing Jesus so wants to give us. We are victors in Him. He has done the work, so now let's walk in it! His cloak covers us; it strengthens and leads us. It is all of Jesus to benefit us at the completeness of His sacrifice to win His children over to Himself. He longs for us to walk in victory and praise. Let's stop dallying in the shallows! Let's walk in the fullness of who God is, follow His plan, and order our steps according to His intricate personal blueprint filled with the good works He planned for each of us. We are in a position to stop the tide of destruction and deception that surrounds the ones we love and threatens to infect their spiritual future.

Let's join together, enter the prayer room, and say, "It is done. It was won on the cross. Jesus' blood covers it all. I am no longer a victim. I am a victor because the blood of Jesus covers everything! He has won the battle, and His cloak is over me, transforming me and fitting me for my heavenly home. He will not desert me, He has not forgotten me, nor will he ever forsake me."

Bank on His promises, and walk in the strength of His power alone. To Him be all the glory—hallelujah!

> On the very night when Herod was about to bring him forward, Peter was sleeping between two soldiers, bound with two chains, and guards in front of the door were watching over the prison. And behold, an angel of the Lord suddenly appeared and a light shone in the cell; and he struck Peter's side and woke him up, saying, "Get up quickly," And his chains fell off his hands. And the angel said to him, "Gird yourself and put on your sandals." And he did so. And he said to him, "Wrap your cloak around you and follow me." And he went out and continued to follow, and he did not know that what was being done by the angel was real, but thought he was seeing a vision. (Acts 12:6–9)

God covers us with His cloak, with the totality of His power and grace, and reminds us who we are in Him. We have all the resources we need to fight the good fight. It all rests with God, who at the cross threw His cloak of unconditional love and forgiveness over us. When we are called into battle, we cannot do it in our own strength, but we must be girded with the cloak of the Lord. Covered by the blood of Christ, we are protected by His hand and empowered by the majestic glory that covers Him on the throne. We must walk in it, trust in it, and lean hard into it. His cloak is our covering and protection. Indeed, if God is for us, who can be against us? Don't fear the one who can kill the body, but fear the one who can kill both body and soul. Saints, gather and rise up! Let's claim our inheritance—one of desperate love for Jesus, a singular focus for His glory, and a face set like flint toward heaven. Let nothing deter us from the mission God is laying on our hearts. There is no greater call than to follow a mission of love and reconciliation, a mission of proclamation of the glories of God and His faithfulness, a mission to walk so intimately with our Savior that we move in perfect unison and oneness with Him.

> "Now, my daughter, do not fear. I will do for you whatever you ask, for all my people in the city know that you are a woman of excellence. Now it is true I am a close relative; however, there is a relative closer than I. Remain this night, and when morning comes, if he will redeem you, good; let him redeem you. But if he does not wish to redeem you, then I will redeem you, as the LORD lives. Lie down until morning." So she lay at his feet until morning and rose before one could recognize another; and he said, "Let it not be known that the woman came to the threshing floor." Again he said, "Give me the cloak that is on you and hold it." So she held it, and he measured six measures of barley and laid it on her. Then she went into the city.
> (Ruth 3:11–15)

God does not send us out empty handed. If we will just rest at His feet, He will fill our cloak. He will equip us and empower us, and only then does He send us out.

So beloved one, sit at the feet of your Savior, and seek His heart. Wait for His bidding and His timing. As you wait, take care to walk in obedience and reverence as you follow what He has already revealed. As you abide by His directions, He will fill your cloak even more. He will satisfy you with the totality of His love. He will give the best of grain, the choicest of wines. He truly knows what you need. The riches of His glory are yours, and they will unfold as you sit as His feet and wait for His blessing and His direction. But take heed—the blessing is not for you alone. It is to be poured out as a drink offering to bless all those around you. If you choose to hoard it, God's blessing will cease to flow and multiply. So take heed; seek a deeper devotion, a truer love, and a purer heart that will grow as you rest at His feet.

He calls, "Rest, My child. Walk in what I have revealed, and trust Me for the future."

Know that as you draw near to Him, He will always draw nearer to you! Never forget, you are precious in His sight, and it is His delight to lead and nurture you. He will see you safely home.

# 41

# He's Got You Covered

And Boaz answered and said to her, "All that you have done for your mother-in-law after the death of your husband has been fully reported to me, and how you left your father and mother and the land of your birth, and came to a people that you did not previously know. May the Lord reward your work, and your wages be full from the Lord, the God of Israel, under whose wings you have come to seek refuge." (Ruth 2:11–12)

And he said, "Who are you?" And she answered, "I am Ruth your maid. So spread your covering over you maid, for you are a close relative." (Ruth 3:9)

The cloak of Boaz—it changed Ruth's identity and destination!

She was moved:

From beleaguered to bountiful

Hope was reborn

From lonely to cherished

Needs were supplied

From foreigner to family

Love covered all

From hungry to filled

Future was secured

From famine to feasting

Blessing abounded

From hearsay to heart song

Baby was born

From afflicted to affirmed

Master was delighted

From poor to protected

God provided all

From harshness to kindness

Desperation turned to delightful dependence

From gleaner to one being served

The pagan became an heir!

From forlorn to favor

From outcast to belonging

From refugee to riches

From drudgery to delight

From destitute to delivered

From wailing to rejoicing

From sorrow to inexpressible joy

The abundance of God starts with a decision that cannot be forgotten, deterred, or diminished: "Your people shall be my people and your God, my God." (See Ruth 1:16b.)

How often do we stop to consider all God has saved us from? How often do we regroup to investigate and ponder all He has saved us for? His love is strong and fierce enough to deflect the strongest enemy's dart. His yoke is not cumbersome to wear but gives a freedom that is complete, easy, and delightful because its weight is held by the hand of the Father! His plans will be fulfilled; will you take part in them?

Listen again to the story of Ruth:

*My Boaz:*

*He shelters me,*
*He protects me,*
*He feeds me,*
*He redeems me,*
*He watches over me,*
*He heals me,*
*He directs me,*
*He fills me,*
*He laughs with me,*
*He sings over me,*
*He comforts me,*
*He counsels me,*
*He loves me,*
*He pours His love into me,*
*He corrects me,*
*He gives me His name,*
*His possessions and His life are mine*
*He has thrown His cloak of love over me*
*Nothing can snatch it away,*
*He has given me a future and a hope.*
*I cannot and will not stray—*
*Where else could I find a love like this?*

*—Ruth*

(Do you hear the heart of the Father?)

# 42

# He Is My Covering

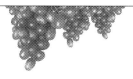

How blessed is he whose transgression is forgiven, whose sin is covered! How blessed is the man to whom the LORD does not impute iniquity, and in whose spirit there is no deceit! (Ps. 32:1–2)

Because he has loved Me, therefore I will deliver him; I will set him securely on high, because he has known My name. He will call upon Me, and I will answer him; I will be with him in trouble; I will rescue him and honor him. With a long life I will satisfy him and let him see My salvation. (Ps. 91:14–16)

When the tempests wail and the winds loudly howl
He is my covering
When the rains turn to torrents and the flood waters rise
He is my covering
When the voice of the accuser overwhelms my senses
He is my covering
When the counsel of others would lead me astray
He is my covering
When my joy seems to fade and my heart grows weaker
He is my covering
When my dreams disturb and my sleep is impaired
He is my covering
When my prayers circle round with no answer found
He is my covering
When my life is confused and wrong appears right
He is my covering
When fights erupt and no peace is in sight

He is my covering
When sin beckons strongly and temptation attacks
He is my covering
When the voice of God grows faint in the midst of the fight
He is my covering
When my calendar crowds Him out of my day
He is my covering
When I am confused and know not what to say
He is my covering
When my words come out twisted and their meaning is muddled
He is my covering
When selfishness rises and a servant's heart flees
He is my covering
When I trust in only the things that I see
He is my covering
When the battle grows fierce and I've fallen again
He is my covering
When my friends turn away and their words sear my heart
He is my covering
When I am confused and don't know where to start
He is my covering
When I give in again to that old, persistent sin
He is my covering
When I fall to my knees, His heart to seek
He is my covering
When I ache over the pain and problems of friends
He is my covering
When I cannot see the pathway or discern its end
He is my covering
When my tears fall silently, unannounced and unwelcome
He is my covering
When confusion steals my peace and leaves me wondering
He is my covering
When truth is obscured and leaves me wandering
He is my covering
When I cry out for wisdom, discernment, and truth
He is my covering

When I lean in close, His heartbeat to hear
He is my covering
And when I pick up the nails to pound into His flesh
Still, He is my covering

# 43

# Mission of the Mind

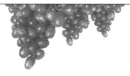

We are destroying speculations and every lofty thing raised up against the knowledge of God, and we are taking every thought captive to the obedience of Christ. (2 Cor. 10:5)

For as he thinks within himself, so he is. (Prov. 23:7a)

But he who is spiritual appraises all things, yet he himself is appraised by no one. For WHO HAS KNOWN THE MIND OF THE LORD, THAT HE WILL INSTRUCT HIM? But we have the mind of Christ. (1 Cor. 2:15–16)

The greatest battles on earth are those fought in the mind. Recognize the competing influences that continually vie for your attention. Take heed as to which voice is tuned in and which one is deflected, for this will largely shape your mental landscape. Cling to that which is true, right, and good, even when circumstances shout at you to believe in the opposite. Where do your thoughts rest and your imaginations dance when you catch yourself daydreaming? This will largely indicate whose voice you are heeding. Seek God and His pleasure. Ask Him to reveal those mental strongholds that are holding you back from the fullness of His love and the outpouring of His purposes in your life.

When your God-sized dreams have started to wither, it is often because the enemy's voice has subtly invaded and turned your attention away from that which is best. If you allow your thoughts to continue in this direction, you will begin to align yourself with the world and its expectations. In doing so, the narrow path appears to grow wider, and slowly but surely, God-sized hope fades into the background. Contentment finds its home with the small, the here and now. The dailies appear so urgent that they smother the gentle call to holiness. Diversion complete, the solider disengages from the vision or dream for the next generation. What legacy are you leaving behind?

What are the building blocks you are using to build up your spiritual house? Are you using intense warfare prayer or the variety that says, "God bless me, Amen"? Are you fasting or feasting? Are you weeping with the things that break God's heart while at the same time rejoicing in His power and His deliverance or pleasuring in the enjoyments of this world? Where does your spirit camp?

Do you see each person, each encounter as divinely orchestrated by God? Will you step into this holy dance and allow God to engage you with those He is pursing? What will you risk to build up for yourself that heavenly treasure that cannot be taken away? Does anyone truly count it all joy when suffering for the sake of righteousness?

How far we all still have to go!

God knows the natural bent toward self: self-satisfaction, self-promotion, self-help, and self-focus. Self, self, self. This is not sweet incense ascending toward the throne. "Greater love has no one than this that one lay down his life for his friends" (John 15:13). Does anyone truly love to this degree or only to the extent to which it is convenient? How helpless we are to love with a God-sized love! Any self-effort will fall sadly short of pleasing God and truly ministering to those we are trying to reach. The mind of Christ—how do we engage it?

We need to cast aside the sin that so easily ensnares us and run the race with endurance. Endurance is a marathon, not just a flashy moment. It is a life built on service and obedience, with each brick and building block sealed with the mortar of God's love. That must be the motive: love. Not heavenly treasure, not counting victories won, not carrying around a warrior's belt with the proverbial heads of those we have won to Christ. Love. Anything done without love is like a clanging cymbal: noisy, abrasive, repelling, and ineffective.

Love is the mind of Christ, for the Father so loved the world that He gave His only begotten Son. (See John 3:16). Love. It is the antidote for self and God's powerful weapon to conquer fear. It is the answer to man's deepest need and desperate cry. His is an unconditional, unconquerable, eternal, powerful, and healing love. How well do we know it? The more we allow God to bathe us in His love, the more we will have to pour out to those around us. We cannot create it on our own; we can only reflect that which we have been so graciously given. "We love because He first loved us" (1 John 4:19).

The mind of Christ is completely inaccessible but for the cross. His cross of suffering and self-denial gives us everything pertaining to righteousness and godliness. This is the cross He calls us to take up daily. We must be dead to self and alive to Christ; alive to His heartbeat, His passions, His mission, and His love. We do not know how the end of the journey will play out on earth, but He does. We may not even know the next step, but He does. He is calling us to walk in the next moment and to build a house of reverent, joyful obedience within our framework of time. Take care of today and hold loosely the plans for tomorrow, all the while asking, "Is what I am doing right now revealing the love of Jesus?" Each time we catch a glimpse of His love pouring out, rejoice, for in this we are becoming more and more aligned with the heartbeat and mind of Christ.

# 44

# Mind of Christ

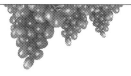

Passion. Imagination. A dream so deep and so far beyond the realm of possibility that the only way to achieve it is to see and walk in the revealed will of God. What are you dreaming? Where have you forgotten how to dream? Where are you bowed down by the pressures of life's trials that have led you to give up on asking God to reveal His heart to move and shake up the situation? Will you dare to ask Him for a fresh understanding and deeper insight into the situation?

> "THINGS WHICH EYE HAS NOT SEEN AND EAR HAS NOT HEARD, AND which HAVE NOT ENTERED THE HEART OF MAN, ALL THAT GOD HAS PREPARED FOR THOSE WHO LOVE HIM." For to us God revealed them through the Spirit; for the Spirit searches all things, even the depths of God. For who among men knows the thoughts of a man except the spirit of the man which is in him? Even so the thoughts of God no one knows except the Spirit of God. Now we have received, not the spirit of the world, but the Spirit who is from God, so that we may know the things freely given to us by God, which things we also speak, not in words taught by human wisdom, but in those taught by the Spirit, combining spiritual thoughts with spiritual words. But a natural man does not accept the things of the Spirit of God, for they are foolishness to him; and he cannot understand them, because they are spiritually appraised. But he who is spiritual appraises all things, yet he himself is appraised by no one. For WHO HAS KNOWN THE MIND OF THE LORD, THAT HE WILL INSTRUCT HIM? But we have the mind of Christ. (1 Cor. 2:9–16)

We have the mind of Christ. What does this mean? Do we appraise things with our human intellect or with our spirit? God does not tell us to lay aside our minds and our intellect but rather to subject them to the leading and lordship of the Holy Spirit. Our mind and our mental gymnastics must come under the lordship and guidance of God. Anything else will be vain imaginations. The longer we marinate in them, the further we will be drawn away from the piercing reality of the truth.

The truth refines, purifies, and stretches our imaginations. It releases the bonds that hold us, and leads us to soar with the hope and promises that God has given His children. You will know the truth because of its ability to set you free! Where are you still walking in bondage? Ask God to reveal a deeper understanding of His truth into that situation. Ask Him for eyes to see as He sees!

Truth without the leading and guidance of the Spirit will eventually lead us into wrong conclusions and suppositions that draw us further away from God. The beginning was good because it began with a grain of truth, but where will it end up? Remember that even the demons masquerade as angels of light. Truth, to be truth, must be able to stand up to the scrutiny of God and the sifting of the Holy Scriptures. It must be able to stand up to the test of time. What truth are you living in that will impact those following you and remain strong throughout the generations? What aroma are you leaving behind you?

The spirit knows the thoughts of a man. As in the order of creation, the created thing in its redeemed state is just a mirror of our God's heart. The way a man's spirit knows his thoughts is a picture of how the Holy Spirit works in unison with the thoughts and intentions of God almighty. This analogy just seems like one more good fact to tuck away into our treasure chest of thoughts. It will not truly impact the way we live unless taken a step deeper.

Paul emphatically stated that we have the mind of Christ. We also have the indwelling of the Holy Spirit. If the spirit knows the thoughts of the man, and if we have the Holy Spirit, then we have access to the thoughts of Christ through the power and direction of the Holy Spirit. Do you catch the depth and richness of this? We have access to the thoughts of God! We are to know what He has freely given to us, and His desire is to share those things with us through the Holy Spirit. We will never understand them if we try to discern them with our natural mind; they must be spiritually discerned.

It is His desire to lead and guide us through to the revealed thoughts of God. Can you catch the potential? We can share in the thoughts of God! This is astonishing, and if we really grab hold of it, it will take away our fear, and our hearts will explode with the joy and thrill of knowing the heart of the Father! This is all given because of the gift of the Holy Spirit and the renewal of our minds through the study of Scripture. The sum of these reveals to us the mind of Christ. We must have both. An over emphasis on either one will leave us unbalanced and prey to attack.

You have the mind of Christ. Grab hold of this; you have the mind of Christ! This is a mystery that is deep and full of promise and potential. The Spirit desires to reveal to you all truths that God has chosen to share. He wants you to know His thoughts and the kind intention of His will. There are also truths that are currently hidden by God. These are not the things to pursue. Leave them with God, trusting Him to expose them at the right time and season.

> In all wisdom and insight He made known to us the mystery of His will, according to His kind intention which He purposed in Him with a view to an administration suitable to the fullness of the times, that is, the summing up of all things in Christ, things in the heavens and things on the earth. (Eph. 1:8b–10)

> For everything created by God is good, and nothing is to be rejected if it is received with gratitude; for it is sanctified by means of the word of God and prayer. (1 Tim. 4:4–5)

# 45

# His Counsel

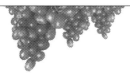

Yet they did not obey or incline their ear, but walked in their own counsels and in the stubbornness of their evil heart, and went backward and not forward. (Jer. 7:24)

You are my hiding place; You preserve me from trouble; You surround me with songs of deliverance. I will instruct you and teach you in the way which you should go; I will counsel you with My eye upon you. (Ps. 32:7–8)

Be strong and very courageous. Be careful to obey all the law my servant Moses gave you; do not turn from it to the right or to the left, that you may be successful wherever you go. (Josh. 1:7)

What a wondrous thought! God counsels you with His eye upon you. He does not just give a command and then leave you to your own resources to figure it out. His eye is on you. He waits, watches, and woos you to respond to His counsel, and as you do, He continues to hold you, to support you, and to direct you. His counsel is open to you not just for the end result, but for each step of the way. He counsels you to incline your ear to the Holy Spirit. He directs you to stay the course, and warns you whenever you are tempted to turn away from the path where He is leading. His counsel is open to all who will hear. It is not limited to a select few. How much do you yearn to hear your Father's voice?

He is directing you to follow His commands, and when you don't first listen, He keeps prodding, keeps speaking, keeps convicting. You have a choice. Will you follow? The more you listen and truly embrace the counsel of God, the clearer and more intimate His voice will become. How well do you know His voice?

If you choose to go your own way, He will let you. He loves you too much to force you to follow Him. Each time you choose your way over His, your hearing grows a little dimmer, your heart a little harder. Continue down this road, and your spiritual hearing will become very dim, until you barely hear Him at all. Darkness will begin to look like light, and deception will crouch at your door, waiting to pounce. You open yourselves up to these perils by your lack of openness to the voice of God through His Holy Spirit.

God in His mercy still yearns for your fellowship, even when you are trying to walk independently of Him. The moment you turn, the minute you confess the hardness of your heart, He runs to you, forgives you, and cleanses you. He draws you back to His heart of love and sets your feet back on the path of righteousness. You will have bruises to heal from and scars from the battle of self-will over God's plan, but these will serve as warning flags for the future. If you take to heart the lessons learned, you will fly higher, with a deeper love for all that God has delivered you from or sustained you through. His compassion will flow into your heart and enable you to reach out to others who are in need of a touch of God's love.

So where are you walking today? Are you leaning on the breast of Jesus to hear His heartbeat, His passions? Or are you quickly running to your own plans and engagements? Listen, saint; listen to the heartbeat of God's love. He will counsel you with His eye upon you, and He will never lead you astray.

# 46

# His Name

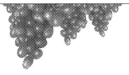

> He makes me lie down in green pastures; He leads me beside quiet waters. He restores my soul; He guides me in the paths of righteousness for His name's sake. (Ps. 23:2–3)

> All the paths of the LORD are lovingkindness and truth to those who keep His covenant and His testimonies. For Your name's sake, O LORD, Pardon my iniquity, for it is great. Who is the man who fears the LORD? He will instruct him in the way he should choose. (Ps. 25:10–12)

What is in a name?

Our name; we are known by it, and we respond to it when called. All of our documents and legal records bear it. It identifies us as who we are and in a way reflects where we have come from, for our parents are the ones who bestowed upon us our name. Our name becomes synonymous with our character, for as people get to know us or know about us, they will hear our name and immediately think, "Oh that person is—fill in the blank—organized, prudent, extravagant, generous, harsh, etc." Our characteristics become associated with our name.

Our name also reflects on our family, our upbringing by our parents, our heritage, and those qualities that we pass down to our children. By our name we can be known as the community-minded people, the athletic people, those who are blessed with great intellect, or those who are prudent or wise. Our names reflect who we are, where we have come from, and where we are going.

However, when we meet Christ for the first time as our Savior, our name is forever changed. We are no longer bound by the past because He wipes it clean. Our destiny has been changed, and our identity becomes enveloped in who He is, God! No longer are our only resources bound up in our own strength, wisdom, and intellect or reputation—our name—but we have the full resources of heaven available to us through Christ's blood, and they await our discovery.

We belong to Christ. He is ours, and we are His. He has made us coheirs with Him. Amazing! Our new name is "coheir with Christ," and we must embrace this fully. Yet, in our earth-bound state, we have the tendency to try and appropriate heaven's resources for our own benefit. We run to Jesus when we are hurt, when we are confused, and when we are perplexed to seek His help and aid. This is right and good, but we need to move in a little closer, a little deeper. Why do we have these resources available to us? We have them because of Christ and because we belong to Him. He cares for us. He knows our needs before we ask, and He promises to provide all of our needs according to the riches of His glory in Christ Jesus. But is this the end of the story?

We come to God on the basis of relationship. We are His children, and we have been redeemed by the blood of Christ. He has a huge investment in us—the life of His Son! We now bear His name, and we are filled with His Spirit. Our new name is "belongs to Christ." No longer do our actions just reflect on our earthly family; they reflect on God Himself!

When we cry to God for help, a breathless wonder swirls about us in the spirit realm. Our enemies tempt us to question if He will respond, the angels await His bidding, and the saints rest in assurance that He will answer. It is God's reputation at stake. Is He able? He hears us because we are His. He answers and meets our needs. In the process, a bit more of His glory and power are revealed upon this earth-bound realm. It is *His reputation* that goes forth, and *His name* that is esteemed as His benevolent answers pour down from the throne.

So, saint, do you approach the throne of grace just on the basis of your need alone? Or will you take it one step further and ask God to help you so that His name can be proclaimed and His righteousness revealed through you in the way that He answers? Self-focused or God-centered prayer—the choice is yours.

> Let this be the reward of my accusers from the LORD, and of those who speak evil against my soul. But You, O GOD, the Lord, deal kindly with me for Your name's sake; because Your lovingkindness is good, deliver me; for I am afflicted and needy, and my heart is wounded within me. (Ps. 109:20–22)

> Incline Your ear to me, rescue me quickly; be to me a rock of strength, a stronghold to save me. For You are my rock and my fortress; For Your name's sake You will lead me and guide me. You will pull me out of the net which they have secretly laid for me, for You are my strength. (Ps. 31:2-4)

# 47

# Longing for God

And as Jesus returned, the people welcomed Him, for they had all been waiting for Him. (Luke 8:40)

The level of our longing for Jesus will deeply impact how much we welcome Him, even in those unplanned visits and interruptions. Is our longing for Him so intense that when He shows up, we run to Him and embrace Him? Is it so fierce that we drop our plans and follow Him wherever He wants to lead? Or are we stuck in our present pattern of behavior and will only welcome Him when He fits into our well-designed box—a box that has no chance of erupting with the power and might of God because its boundaries are determined by our own level of ability and talent?

Do we long for God more than the physical comforts we spend our life pursuing? How much do we really thirst for a new vision, a new revelation, a new movement of the hand of God? Woe to us when we are content to keep walking in today's path and pattern. The level of our spiritual contentment is inversely proportional to the intenseness of God's fire and passion that we will be privileged to share in our earth-bound days. It will also affect our ability to bear new fruit for the kingdom. God births a new vision. He draws the pieces into place so they fit like a well-crafted and carefully-designed puzzle. It is our choice whether we will be included in this master work of His hand. How much do we long for Him? How much do we desire to see a fresh move, a new fire of God fall down? *Our welcome of Jesus will only be as deep and focused as the intensity of our waiting for Him.*

So how do we thirst for more of God? Can this be self-manufactured within our own spirit? No, we cannot even do this. We must fall before the

Lord almighty and beseech Him to reignite our passion and our hunger for Him. He is the spark that lights the bonfire within our souls. He brings the kindling that will catch fire. He is the one who hauls in the logs to keep the fire burning brighter, hotter, and with an ever-increasing intensity and purity. All we need to do is to present to Him a clear fire pit. We need to embrace Him and turn from the sin that so easily traps us. As the sparks begin to sputter and the flames of a godly passion begin to catch, guard the perimeter of your fire pit. Do not let the enemy's impurities and junk get thrown into the fire. The beauty is that even when those half-truths—those twisted perceptions—threaten to crowd in, the fire of God is so hot, so pure, and so full of a cleansing power that as we yield to the fire of His love, we will be freed and cleansed from all impurities and all that is unholy.

So how much do you long for God today? Will you continue to wait for Him? The longer the wait, the sweeter and deeper the reward, and the more precious His presence will become!

# 48

# Jesus Cares

These things I have spoken to you, so that in Me you may have peace. In the world you have tribulation, but take courage; I have overcome the world. (John 16:33)

Beloved, do not believe every spirit, but test the spirits to see whether they are from God, because many false prophets have gone out into the world. By this you know the Spirit of God: every spirit that confesses that Jesus Christ has come in the flesh is from God; and every spirit that does not confess Jesus is not from God; this is the spirit of the antichrist , of which you have heard that it is coming, and now it is already in the world. You are from God, little children, and have overcome them; because greater is He who is in you than he who is in the world. (1 John 4:1–4)

Jesus cares
I hurt
Jesus cares
I'm confused
Jesus cares
I'm dismayed
Jesus cares
I can't seem to move forward
Jesus cares
I'm angry and mad

Jesus cares
I'm full of sorrow
Jesus cares
I'm worried about tomorrow
Jesus cares
My prayers seem to hit the ceiling
Jesus cares
I'm only going through the motions
Jesus cares
I'm so frustrated
Yet Jesus still cares
Jesus cares
I've lost hope
Jesus cares
I feel so alone
Jesus cares
Jesus cares
Jesus cares
But He won't leave me there
He keeps wooing
He keeps calling
And He keeps drawing me back
Until I see Him
He's opened my eyes
I've found peace
I've found rest
I've found purpose
I've found passion
I finally know I am fully loved
I've been convicted
And I've been cleansed
All because Jesus cares

# 49

# I Am

You are never alone,
Though you pass through the valley of the shadow of death, I am there,
Though tempests surround you, threaten to overwhelm you, I am there,
Though your loved one has disappointed you again, I am there,
Though you grow weary and tired and feel you can't go on, I am there,
I am there, through the ups and downs, the disappointments, the
    heartache and the joy,
I am there.

I will comfort you,
I will counsel you,
I will hold you in perfect peace.
If you will only look to Me,
I am there.

My wisdom is big enough,
My arms are long enough,
My understanding is deep enough.
Will you trust Me?

I Am that I Am,
I am your song in the night,
I am your light in the day,
I am in the dearest dreams you hold close to your heart,
I am the arms that hold you close,
I am your counselor and comforter.

I Am.
I Am.
I Am.

I am your peace that passes understanding,
I am your hope in the storm,
I am your joy that comes in the morning,
I am the hope that will not die,
I am holding you close,
I am the Author of all life.
Can you feel my love?

I Am
I Am
I Am

I am your helper and provider,
I am the giver of all good things,
I am the Spirit who leads and guides you,
I am the one who sends my angels to minister and guide,
I am righteous one who loves you,
I am the Holy One who has redeemed you.

I Am
I Am
I Am

I will never leave nor forsake you,
I hear your unspoken cry,
I understand the depth of your sorrow,
I am the only One who holds tomorrow,
I will carry you through each moment,
And I will see you safely home.
All because,

I Am

To which of the angels did God ever say "Sit at my right hand until I make your enemies a footstool for your feet." Are not all angels ministering spirits sent to serve those who will inherit salvation? (Heb. 1:13–14)

So do not throw away your confidence; it will be richly rewarded. You need to persevere so that when you have done the will of God, you will receive what He has promised. (Heb. 10:35–36)

# 50

# Paul's Secret

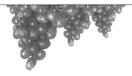

> But I rejoiced in the Lord greatly, that now at last you have
> revived your concern for me; indeed, you were concerned
> before, but you lacked opportunity. Not that I speak from want,
> for I have learned to be content in whatever circumstances I
> am. I know how to get along with humble means, and I also
> know how to live in prosperity; in any and every circumstance
> I have learned the secret of being filled and going hungry, both
> of having abundance and suffering need. I can do all things
> through Him who strengthens me. (Phil. 4:10–13)

Paul had a secret. It sustained him in times of abundance and in times of
utter poverty, in times of peace and in times of intense persecution. He
had that inner peace that the world would look upon and be completely
unable to rationalize away. It truly did pass all understanding. It made no
sense. Here was a man who had been imprisoned, stoned, shipwrecked,
and beaten innumerable times and left as dead. His physical suffering
was also compounded by an intense concern for the welfare of the early
church. He experienced stresses within and deprivation without. How
can a man endure such deep stress and trials? By all rational explanation,
he should have given up and returned to his prior Pharisaical life, where
there was comfort in the familiar and prestige in his heritage. He could
have thrown in the towel and declared that the pursuit of holiness was too
steep, too painful to pursue. Yet he stayed the course and fought the good
fight. What was his secret?

In one word, it was Jesus. He had received a blinding vision (literally!) of
Jesus on the road to Damascus, and he was forever changed. He came face
to face with the Divine One, and suddenly all that he had pursued fell away

as meaningless and worthless. All of his self-righteousness, his works of zeal, his mental prowess concerning the Law; all of it was counted as filthy garbage in comparison with the riches of knowing the Lord Jesus. This is the name above all names, the name at which one day every knee will bow and every tongue will confess that He is Lord. Count on it.

Jesus. It only took one look and Paul's life was forever changed.

So where are you today?

Is your life filled with deep blessings and abundance? Praise the Lord and serve as He leads, just as the Philippians did when the opportunity presented itself to minister to Paul.

Are your resources and finances stretched to the breaking point? Praise the Lord and remember that He clothes even the lilies in beautiful splendor and feeds the birds that have neither sown seed nor harvested the fields. (See Matt. 6:25–34.)

Are you filled with joy and peace? Praise the Lord. Your worship will be contagious and encourage others! They will wonder what your secret is!

Are you shaking with fear, drowning in doubt that He will provide? Look up and praise the Lord. Remember that He is intimately acquainted with all of your ways. He knows your every need and desire, even before you become aware of them. (Ponder that one for a moment and realize the fullness of His grace, His power, His knowledge, and His understanding!) He numbered your days even before there was yet one of them! Can't He then provide for all of your needs within each of those days? (See Ps. 139:16.)

God will meet your every need; His only requirement is that you first seek the kingdom of God. (See Matt. 6:32–33). Is your deepest desire to be relieved of a burden or to be conformed more to the image of Jesus? God is your Jehovah-Jireh, your provider. Are you looking to Him to sustain you and lift your weary head? How intently have you looked into the face of your Savior? Can you say with Paul, "More than that, I count all things to be loss [my successes and failures, my hopes and dreams] in view of the surpassing value of knowing Christ Jesus my Lord, for whom I have suffered the loss of all things, and count them but rubbish so that I may gain Christ" (Phil. 3:8)?

What are you clinging to that is more important than Jesus? Whatever it is, it will become a trap that steals joy and diverts your attention from your King. When you can truly yield all things to God, you will indeed be able to say, "I have learned to be content in all things … because I know my God will never fail me nor forsake me." (See Phil. 4:11 and Deut. 31:6.) He will enable me to go and do whatever He has put before me. It is His power, His love, and His strength that flows through me to accomplish His work. I am only the vessel through which He can pour out His fullness to meet the needs of others. I just need to look to Him and remember that His power, provision, and wisdom will strengthen and support me in everything. I can indeed do *all* things through Christ who strengthens me! (See Phil. 4:13.)

# 51

# Power of Worship

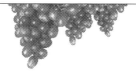

> And the four living creatures, each one of them having six wings, are full of eyes around and within; and day and night they do not cease to say, "HOLY, HOLY, HOLY is THE LORD GOD, THE ALMIGHTY, WHO WAS AND WHO IS AND WHO IS TO COME." And when the living creatures give glory and honor and thanks to Him who sits on the throne, to Him who lives forever and ever, the twenty-four elders will fall down before Him who sits on the throne, and will worship Him who lives forever and ever, and will cast their crowns before the throne, saying, "Worthy are You, our Lord and our God, to receive glory and honor and power; for You created all things, and because of Your will they existed, and were created." (Rev. 4:8–11)

Notice that the four living creatures do not cease to worship. If they who are so close to God exist in continual worship, shouldn't we as God's redeemed be doing the same thing? This leads one to ponder if the prompting of our worship unto the King of Kings might be birthed through the worship of the four living creatures. If so, as their worship is constant, so must ours be! They worship Him day and night; do we?

True, pure worship emanates from our spirits under the guidance of the Holy Spirit. It does not come from our natural minds, for then when our minds and bodies grow weary, the worship wanes. If our spirits are fueled by the worship of the four living creatures, we should have the capacity to worship with all our being. These creatures who are before the throne of God have eyes in front and behind (v. 6), and therefore they are able to behold the fullness of the glory of God. As they behold the glory of God, their only possible response is to continually worship the King!

This worship birthed in the throne room of God has wings to fly, and it gladly worships that which is true about God. It worships to a degree of fullness and completeness that we can only at this point vaguely imagine. Throne room worship is adoration born of the Spirit. It is free and exuberant and multiplies itself so we can begin to worship day and night. Think of King David, unrobed and dancing in the street unto his God as the ark of the Lord was returned to Jerusalem. (See 2 Sam. 6:14–23.) That is exuberant worship! As we begin to reach up and seek God for a more full, a more complete type of worship, we will begin to experience just a taste of the worship offered by the four living creatures, and our worship will grow into that which is continuous!

Worship that is directed by the mind will only reach up as far as we can see or understand. It is limited by our earth-bound limitations. Worship birthed in the Spirit has no boundaries and is free to fly wherever the Holy Spirit directs. Too often we are stuck in the worship of mental assent limited by our concrete, earthly focused minds. Worship rooted in our flesh and emotions is easily sidetracked and knocked off course by distractions and wandering thoughts. Worship birthed under the guidance of the Spirit rises up like an effervescent stream that continues to bubble up and refresh us with the glory of the Lord.

Continue to ponder the worship of the four living creatures. Could their worship fuel and prompt the hearts of those who will listen carefully? Their songs echo in the corners of our souls, for we were reborn through Jesus' blood to fly with the Spirit in the courtyards of our King! Our worship will take on a deeper and purer form if we will learn to listen and respond to the promptings of the Holy Spirit. The creatures worship God because they behold Him in all His glory and because of what they see in the throne room of heaven. Although their worship can fuel our worship, *our worship is unique according to our identity.* They worship because they see God's glory. We have so much more! By Christ's blood, we are coheirs with Christ, and through His atonement, we are children of the King. Because God sent the Holy Spirit at Pentecost, we also have the Holy Spirit residing within us as our seal of adoption. Since we have the Spirit of God, our worship, although fueled and prompted by the worship of the four living creatures, is unique from theirs. As His children, our worship is birthed *not by sight but in the very heart of God!*

If this is your heart's desire, please pray along with me:

> Lord, I want to worship You with the spirit of heaven. Please change me, alter my focus, and fill me with the glories due to You and Your throne. Let it flow out of me like living water, and may I hold nothing back. May everything in me be all for Your glory and honor, now and forever!

# 52

# Praise Fest

> Why are you in despair, O my soul? And why have you become disturbed within me? Hope in God, for I shall again praise Him for the help of His presence. (Ps. 42:5)

> Why are you in despair, O my soul? And why have you become disturbed within me? Hope in God, for I shall yet praise Him, the help of my countenance and my God. (Ps. 42:11)

> Why are you in despair, O my soul? And why are you disturbed within me? Hope in God, for I shall again praise Him, the help of my countenance and my God. (Ps. 43:5)

When is the last time you came before God with no other agenda, but to praise Him?

How often have you willingly laid aside your laundry list of prayer requests and just come to sit at His feet?

Do you know how to sit with Jesus and just enjoy His love?

All too often we get bogged down by the pain and trials of this earth. We diligently try to hold them up to the throne of grace, but as we hold them up with arms of our own understanding, we quickly grow weary and eventually quit. Our heart's desire is to persevere, to see the glory of God fall down and minister and heal and set things right. If we do this in our own power, our own understanding, according to our own time (*now!*), we will quickly tire and give up. What can give us the fuel to carry on, to push through, and to overcome the discouragement that so quickly threatens to undo us?

## God-Centered Praise

We will give up if we do not hope in the glory of the Lord. We must come back again and again and again to the throne room of the King. We must pause in our mad dash. We must stop and lay aside the sunglasses of this world that blind us to the glory of the King. We must enter His courts with thanksgiving and praise even when—especially when—things look the darkest and most bleak. God will truly accomplish all that concerns us. When did we stop believing this and cease from walking in the hope of its fulfillment? *When we stopped praising Him and believing His Word!*

Our dreams and our hopes are way too small. How we limit Him by our lack of a godly viewpoint and imagination. Where has our mustard seed of faith been drowned out by too much doubt and unbelief? When did we forget how to dream, how to truly hope in God? When did we give up and start to tough it out on our own? When did we choose to ignore the magnitude of God's power? When did our focus shift? Do you know often Jesus cries over us, "Oh, you of little faith"? Hope yet again in God, and we will behold the magnificence of His glory!

As a parent, how often do we repeat ourselves to get our point across? Shouldn't we perk up and listen when God repeats Himself? Do you think He is trying to get our attention? (Notice the repeated theme in the above verses.)

> For the LORD is righteous, He loves righteousness; The upright will behold His face. (Ps. 11:7)

> Forever, O LORD, Your word is settled in heaven. Your faithfulness continues throughout all generations; You established the earth, and it stands. They stand this day according to Your ordinances, For all things are Your servants. If Your law had not been my delight, Then I would have perished in my affliction. I will never forget Your precepts, For by them You have revived me. I am Yours, save me; For I have sought Your precepts. The wicked wait for me to destroy me; I shall diligently consider Your testimonies. I have seen

a limit to all perfection; Your commandment is exceedingly broad. (Ps. 119:89–96)

Oh how the moments of life's experience resonate with God's truth! I am reminded once again of the impact of words and am humbled by all the empty words I have spoken. May God touch our lips with the burning coal from the glory of His presence and cleanse, purify, and anoint everything about us, including our words!

# 53

# Words of Salt

The scribes and the Pharisees brought a woman caught in adultery, and having set her in the center of the court, they said to Him, "Teacher, this woman has been caught in adultery, in the very act. Now in the Law Moses commanded us to stone such women; what then do You say?" They were saying this, testing Him, so that they might have grounds for accusing Him. But Jesus stooped down and with His finger wrote on the ground. But when they persisted in asking Him, He straightened up, and said to them, "He who is without sin among you, let him be the first to throw a stone at her." Again He stooped down and wrote on the ground. When they heard it, they began to go out one by one, beginning with the older ones, and He was left alone, and the woman, where she was, in the center of the court. Straightening up, Jesus said to her, "Woman, where are they? Did no one condemn you?" She said, "No one, Lord." And Jesus said, "I do not condemn you, either. Go. From now on sin no more." (John 8:3–11)

Advice without compassion and counsel without solicitation leave feelings of deflation, discouragement, and often defeat. How ironic; this is the exact opposite of what the speaker intended when offering his brand of comfort. We tend to quickly offer our perspective and words of advice. How different our interactions would be if we would figuratively stoop to draw in the sand before rising to address those before us. In those times of what may appear to mindless dawdling, if we are truly listening to the heartbeat of heaven, we will receive insight and revelation appropriate for the moment. How often do we really stop to receive a God-breathed word?

Salt is essential and necessary to cleanse wounds and preserve and protect that which is good. But there must be the appropriate entry point for these words of salt. We need to learn to rejoice with those who rejoice and weep with those who weep, even in those minute circumstances that are not earth shattering or life altering. Even in the small details of life, if we are not careful, we will step on toes and offend rather than encourage in our effort to counsel and equip the saints. Never assume that you know the complete picture of what another is experiencing. Your experience may be similar, but the road for each travel-weary saint is as unique and varied as the shadows of sunlight dancing through wind-tossed branches. The best that our common life journey can offer is a heart bathed in compassion and mercy.

As we reach out with the loving arms of Jesus, we must listen more and counsel less. As we tune into the heart of another, we must be simultaneously listening for the quiet voice the Holy Spirit to lead and guide us as to the truth needed in that exact moment. The counsel waiting to burst from our lips may be theologically sound, but if it is not bathed in the love and compassion of Jesus, it will fall flat on the ground and miss its intended mark, the heart's passion of the hearer. This is the challenge of any teacher to share the truth in a way that will not compromise its central message but be effective to reach the target of the listener's heart. We need to appropriate Paul's teaching to become all things to all men so that we might reach some. Only God's grace can pave the way. We will only learn to walk in this way as we are in continual communication with our Father. We must seek Him often for a new measure and filling of His love so we do not become those clanging cymbals and noisy gongs that grate and do little more than irritate.

There will be times when God calls on us to speak a hard word. Proceed with much caution and prayer. We must be careful to take the log out of our own eye before attempting to minister to the sliver in a friend's line of vision. Remember, God knows exactly what they need, and He is able to meet them perfectly in their current state. We may be honored with the joy of sharing in the Father's work. Do not handle this privilege lightly. Our words carry the power of both life and death. Strive to always speak words of life, not empty flattery or shallow encouragement but life words.

Words can see into the spirit of a man and lift his vision up to the throne of grace. These words are those that are birthed in the throne room of heaven. We will only be able to appropriate them, their content and timeliness, if we have trained our ears to listen to the counsel of the Holy Spirit. The admonition to be quick to hear and slow to speak has deep merit for the life of the saint. God will equip us in our life journey to be that listening ear and seeing eye. How He desires to pour the completeness of His love into our spirits. He knows that as we experience a fuller measure of His boundless love, our perception will be unalterably changed, and our lives will begin to flow with a fuller measure of grace.

Precious one, let Him love on you in your deepest point of need. Reach up and cry out to God, and know He hears your deepest heart's cry. As the mercy of God floods your spirit, you will then be better equipped to reach out and offer His living water to others walking the journey of faith. Waste nothing, but yield everything up to your Lord and Savior. Praise Him for His abundant love. Worship Him, for He alone is worthy. As you stand upon His truth and counsel you will be amazed at the change in your perspective and how the depth of love for your God begins to flourish. The more you seek after God and let Him bathe you in His love, the more the glory of His love will flow from your spirit. You will begin to radiate with God's divine presence, and His love will move to change and impact your world. Many will see, some will understand, others will begin their search for God, and some will mock. Do not be deterred. Keep running hard after God, and always seek to love with a God-sized love. Anything less will miss the mark.

# 54

# The Old Order

> And I heard a loud voice from the throne, saying, "Behold the tabernacle of God is among men, and He will dwell among them, and they shall be His people, and God Himself will be among them, and He will wipe away every tear from their eyes; and there will no longer be any death; there will no longer be any mourning, or crying, or pain; the first things have passed away. (Rev. 21:3–4)

One need only look around to acknowledge that we currently live in a world filled with suffering and pain. All creation yearns and groans under the weight of sin. We are tossed about within by our own doubts and fears and are buffeted without by a godless culture that appears to be running headlong away from God and full tilt into a deeper and more desperate depravity. Oh, who can free us from this body of death? Praise God that the full work of redemption was done on the cross over two thousand years ago. Jesus paid the awful price to forgive us our sin, and He gives the only freedom that will last—one that cannot be stripped away. We have the fullness of freedom in Him. He gives hope when despair threatens to undo us. He gives strength when our weaknesses submerse us. His understanding and wisdom pierce the darkest night, and His love covers a multitude of sins.

How we long for that day when there will be no more mourning or crying or pain. In this, we too join with creation and groan for our ultimate day of liberation and full freedom to embrace all of God. But for now we are each called to walk in a world filled with suffering and pain. We are called to be the hands and feet of Jesus to those in need. This is an incredible witness and ministry to touch the lives of those who are suffering. It is one in which we are all called to serve. We are to dwell with Jesus in the secret places to gather the fuel, love, and motive to serve as He would serve and to love as He would love.

How do we continue on this path day after day and year after year without growing weary and giving up? It is by looking forward to that wonderful day when there will be no more crying and pain, no more death or mourning. As we pour out all that Jesus has given us, He will continue to pour in and sustain and strengthen us. Yet He also challenges us, in the middle of this battle, to go one step further. Will we choose to worship Him in the midst of the struggle and pain? As we worship right in the thickest part of the battle, we acknowledge that this present order of things has no power over us, because we belong to the King. Our worship testifies that this present order will soon pass away, never to be seen again. The sin that so easily entangles us has been dealt its death blow at the cross.

As we lean hard into Jesus and worship Him for who He is, the power and strength of sin is loosened, and its hold of torment and anguish is crushed. Our spirits are free to exault the King, no matter where we are or how deep the trial. As we worship, we are joining with the angelic voices proclaiming the coming day of the Lord. We unite with the voice of heaven to proclaim that Christ is indeed King and we are His people—forever! This old order has no power over us. We live in it but do not need to succumb to it, for we are destined for a higher glory. As we choose to worship and rejoice even in the midst of dark pain, we are proclaiming the coming of our King and the New Jerusalem. Let us worship Him in all things and so proclaim His sufficiency and power to break the hold of this present order. He dwells within us and tabernacles with us through the Holy Spirit. Will we acknowlege Him and reverence Him through our praise?

# 55

# Out with the Old

Shed off your old clothes.
Take on the glory of God.
Walk in newness of today, not sameness of yesterday.
Ask for a fresh filling, anointing, a new flow of the Holy Spirit.
Earnestly seek after the wisdom and counsel of God in all things.
Stop leaning on your own understanding.
Ask for God's vision and His heart.
Walk in it!

We have been feasting on the crumbs of God's table,
And it has been incredible.
He is now calling us to move into a new place.
Come join Him at His banquet feast!
Will you hunger for more of Him?
For a deeper knowledge?
A knowing and being known?
A joy so deep that it takes your breath away?
Breathless with the wonder, excitement, and awe of an Almighty God!

This knowledge does not just edify the mind,
But it burns so deeply within the soul,
That nothing else will ever be the same.
Are we willing to take off yesterday's clothes?
Are we thirsting for a fresh move of God?
Is the thirst so deep that nothing else will satisfy?
Will you choose a settled life,
One routine with your own plans and designs,
Or one vibrant, alive, and pulsing with the heartbeat of God?

Will fear stop you?
What about the lure of acceptance?
Would you rather be applauded by men,
Or bring joy to your Savior?
Who are you following, and where are you walking?
A sane and safe path,
Or one filled with the vibrant, pulsating unknowingness,
Of following the one we do not yet fully know?
Take heart; you are completely known!

Join me today.
Cast off the sameness of yesterday.
Keep the lessons learned.
Worship through the victories won,
Then leave them at the altar.
Turn your face toward heaven,
And your heart toward home.
The Spirit is stirring the embers in your spirit.
Let Him have His way!

Do not quench the fire.
Can you feel it? It's beginning to grow.
Lean into it, grab hold of it, and ask for more!
Your Father will not give you a stone!
Will you trust Him to finish what He has begun?
Will you question His work or deny His call?
Hear the call to walk deeper with Him.
There is an urgency—there is no time to waste!
Come join the pulse beat of heaven!

Welcome the refreshing waters of His Spirit!
Will the mystery of it all draw you or repulse you?
There are no hiding holes when we walk honestly with God!
Lay it all back down on the altar,
And welcome His cleansing fire!
It will pierce and wound,
But it is a piercing unto wholeness,
And we will never be the same.
Hallelujah!

# 56

# Heart of the Matter

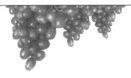

*Read Jeremiah 3:6–11.*

> And the Lord said to me, "Faithless Israel has proved herself more righteous than treacherous Judah." (Jer. 3:11)

Are your acts of piety for your own reputation or God's?

Are you zealous for how others perceive you or for God's presence to radiate through you to the point that you become invisible to others and all they see is Jesus?

Do you engage in lip service or heart's devotion?

Are you willing to ask God to show you where you have been faithless to Him?

Have you counted the cost of yielding everything to Jesus?

Beware when your lips speak the truth of God but your heart is far removed from it!

Ask the Lord to be your judge now, while there is time to repent!

Ask God to align your passions with those that warm His heart!

**A God-Ordained Shift**
False piety goes for the show.
Holy dependence produces a glow.
Those far off will be called near.
Their broken lives to God are so dear.

He calls us go, reach out to the lost,
For they by sin's sway have been ravaged and tossed.
Their hope grows dimmer day by day.
They hunger for truth but know not what to say.

They are clueless as to where they should seek,
So they exalt the proud and revile the meek.
They continue on in the path they have hewn,
Oblivious to truth that has so liberally been strewn.

Through the pages of this Holy Book,
God is calling them to come and take a look.
But their hearts have been hardened by relentless sin,
That swirls and beckons and draws them further in.

Deeper and darker their sin stain grows,
All because the truth they do not know.
God's people have held it close to their hearts,
And refused His call to go and depart.

Out from their fellowship so divine and sweet,
To go to the broken and wash their feet.
To make themselves as nothing for the sake of the lost,
We talk and we pray, but have we counted the cost,

Of ignoring God's heart that seeks to save?
We've been given the truth their way to pave.
A pathway to heaven so simple and pure,
A salvation that is free, guaranteed and insured.

By the matchless blood of Jesus shed for all.
Saints, will we follow and heed His call?
He will try us and sift us, and our hearts will surely break,
As He pours in His holiness to our affections remake.

To be Jesus' hands, His heart and His feet,
Let us rise up now and go out to the street.
To draw in those who are suffering and wandering away,
From the love of a Savior who bids them to stay.

Close to His heart that will shelter and guide,
And give them peace if they will only abide,
In the covenant of grace won by the cross.
For its glory we must count everything loss.

And reach out to those hurting, deceived, and blind.
We hold the truth, will we pay them any mind?
And offer that cup of living water so sweet.
It soothes the parched soul that seems bound for defeat.

This water not only saves from the sorrows of today,
But it wins them for heaven, where forever they will stay.
Once they have come to Jesus for cleansing and hope,
And we will stand in glory rejoicing because we threw them the rope!

> Then I will give you shepherds after My own heart; who will
> feed you on knowledge and understanding. (Jer. 3:13)

# 57

# Danger of Familiarity

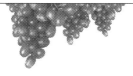

Yet for this reason I found mercy, so that in me as the foremost, Jesus Christ might demonstrate His perfect patience as an example for those who would believe in Him for eternal life. (1 Tim. 1:16)

Then one of the synagogue leaders, named Jairus, came, and when he saw Jesus, he fell at His feet. He pleaded earnestly with Him, "My little daughter is dying. Please come and put Your hands on her so that she will be healed and live. So Jesus went with him. (Mark 5:22–24)

Does Jesus go with you? We know from Isaiah 52:12 and Psalm 91:10-12 that He is our leader and rear guard and He gives His angels charge concerning us to keep us from striking our foot upon a stone. We know these things, and we rejoice in them. We know we are covered and protected by the hand of God, and that brings much comfort and solace, especially in times of testing, temptation, or trial. But when we are not in those types of dire circumstances, our tendency is to treat the Holy One with an attitude of familiarity; Jesus met me there, He will meet me again. It is familiarity without reverence that leads us astray.

After developing a life history with Jesus, it is natural to treat Him as our best friend. But in this intimacy, it is easy to forget that He is almighty God, and as the Supreme One, all honor and glory is His due. Do we really fall at His feet to worship and adore Him *before* we bring our petitions to Him? It is so easy to approach the throne of grace in an effort to relieve ourselves of pain. Truly we are not burden-bearing animals, and it is Jesus' pleasure to draw close as we reach up to Him. Oh how He loves His sheep! He tells us to come to Him when we are weary and heavy laden. As we lift our soul-weary prayers up to the throne of grace, He gently bows down to wipe off our muddy faces so we can see His heart of love more clearly. As we catch a purer glimpse of His grace covering us in the place of divine intervention, we do indeed find a rest that is beyond our human understanding. For a moment a holy hush falls upon the soul as we behold the magnificence of the Almighty parting the seas of affliction to rescue His storm-tossed child. However, when the waves subside, life begins to once again demand our attention. We engage with the daily routine and quickly forget those moments of complete surrender. Yet, for just a moment, the mortal beheld the divine and in the process was changed.

Answered prayer affirms to our hearts that we are indeed children of the King. We rejoice in our relationship and come to depend on its benefits. Experience can be a wonderful teacher or a cruel task master, depending on how we handle our memories. As we collect more and more God stories, our capacity for joy will increase and fill the barren spots in our souls. We sing and praise because God has met us in the hard place. It is easy to be spontaneous with praise when He has delivered us or empowered us to walk through a difficulty. Yet when our worship is driven by our circumstances, it is transitory at best and can be swayed when the next storm comes—that is, unless we hold tightly to the memory of God's assistance and extrapolate truths from that intervention to remind us of His unchangeable ways and holy nature.

In those moments of victorious joy, we cannot see the next obstacle around the bend, waiting and ready to assail our faith. God sees it, and He knows how we will respond. Will it be with cries of desperation for deliverance or with hands lifted high to extol the character of God because we have seen His faithfulness in the past? When we are staring conflict in the face, do we run whimpering into the throne room? Or will we stand on the shoulders of our God-inspired memories and proclaim His goodness and faithfulness even before we bring our petitions to His feet? As we determine to worship Him with every memory and each moment, our worship will grow unfettered and free. It will fill our waking moments and dance through the courts of our dreams. It will color the flavor of our prayer life and make our faith infectious, all because we chose to worship in the hard place and offer thanksgiving as a forerunner to our petitions.

As our worship, adoration, and reverence grow, so too will our ability to radiate with the light and glory of God. His love will become more intimate and precious. We possess all this because in the midst of our pain, we chose to worship and adore before we sought after God's hand for our deliverance.

# 58

# Worshipping Warrior

> Therefore let us leave the elementary teachings about Christ and go on to maturity, not laying again the foundation of repentance from acts that lead to death, and of faith in God, instruction about baptisms, the laying on of hands, the resurrection of the dead, and eternal judgment. And God permitting, we will do so. … Even though we speak like this, dear friends, we are confident of better things in your case—things that accompany salvation. God is not unjust; He will not forget your work and the love you have shown Him as you have helped His people and continue to help them. We want each of you to show this same diligence to the very end, in order to make your hope sure. We do not want you to become lazy, but to imitate those who through faith and patience inherit what has been promised. (Heb. 6:1–3, 9–12)

God is the God of hope. He will not forget anything you have done for Him on behalf of His people. Keep on keeping on, saint, and you will receive your reward. God will not let go of any of the good works you have done. They are all treasured up in heaven, waiting for you. Once you pass from this mortal life into the eternal, you will cast your crowns at the feet of Jesus and worship Him even more fully because of the work of service you have rendered here in this time and place. Flee the temptation to work for what is perishable and momentary. Push forward toward that which is eternal and pleasing in God's sight. All that you achieve is only possible because God first planted the desire in your spirit and then equipped you with the ability, strength, and resources to accomplish that task for Him—all to His glory!

God works out His plans in the routine of your life to increasingly conform you into the image of His Son. When your cries to heaven align with that purpose, He is delighted to bend down and meet you, even at times while you are still in the moment of prayer! Let's join together and seek after God's heart.

Cleanse me, oh Lord—and I will be clean and whiter than snow!
Change me, oh Lord—and I shall be changed and made new.
Heal me, oh Lord—and I shall be healed with a song of praise.
Comfort me, oh Lord—and I shall be met with a comfort so deep that
    its impact will be boundless.
Instruct me, oh Lord—and I shall learn to walk in Your ways of wisdom.
Surround me, oh Lord—and I shall be protected and held tight in the
    midst of the battle.
Shine on me, oh Lord—and I shall radiate Your glory into the darkness
    infecting this world.

Your growth into all things holy depends on God's mercy and grace. All He requires of you is to ask Him, seek Him, and respond to Him. The battle is the Lord's; give it back to Him. Wait for His marching orders! Rest in the knowledge, dear one, that nothing you do for your precious King is wasted. He sees it all and knows the depth and sincerity of your heart. God does not measure you by your successes, for He is the one who brings the bud to blossom and bear fruit through the passion and integrity of your heart.

He sees, He knows, and He understands your frustration and your pain. He knows where you are weary and ready to give up. Run to Him and He will refresh and rearm you for the battle. The only thing He calls you to give up is your dream for the future in exchange for His divine plan specifically tailored for you. This plan was formed before you first saw the light of day. It is so much greater and grander that it puts all earth-bound plans to shame! So lean into Him, listen for His still, sweet voice, and be refreshed and reassured that all you do for the sake of the kingdom will not be forgotten. Continue walking in His grace, and one sweet day you will hear, "Well done, faithful servant, come into your rest!" (See Matt. 25:21.)

Learn to walk in the Ws:

- Worship—God for who He is!

- Wait—for your guidance and instructions from the throne room.

- War—Go courageously into the battle where God is calling, in His time!

- Worship—giving thanks, glory, and honor to the King of Kings for all He has done!

This is the mind-set and focus of a worshipping warrior. May God further lead us each into the depth of truth and reveal to us the pivotal role of worship!

# 59

# Who Knows You?

Search me, O God, and know my heart; try me and know my anxious thoughts; and see if there be any hurtful way in me, and lead me in the everlasting way. (Ps. 139:23–24)

We all readily acknowledge that we are sinners in need of a Savior. The evidence is rampant, and there is no denying that we daily need cleansing and purifying. Consider how we go about the purification process, for this reveals the state of the union inside our own hearts. Do we first sit down and peruse the landscape of our hearts and spirits and blindly throw up everything to the throne of grace that appears unworthy of being called a child of God? At first glance, this seems like a noble thing to do—even the right thing to do. But if we will stop and take a closer look, this method merits further scrutiny. If our focus is to seek our own hearts, Scripture in essence says we are at best deluded and unwise, for the heart of man is sinful. Who can know it? (See Jer. 17:9.)

Who are we to think that we know what is wrong inside our spirits? What tremendously arrogant pride it is to presume that we fully know ourselves! Yet isn't this what we do every day? If we are honest and truly look at our internal landscape, we see that the immediate reflex is to defend our positions—to move things into place so we look good. Our innate response is to justify our attitudes and reactions and occasionally to throw the whole mess up to God to ask for cleansing. But when we engage in this type of activity, our thought process is in reality proclaiming that we, not God, are the author and sharpener of our faith. It says, in essence, that we know what is wrong within ourselves, and we only need ask God's forgiveness to get everything set right again. This in its basest sense is the root of all pride, thinking that we know ourselves this well. God forgive us!

*Jan Hegelein*

When we attempt to analyze our own spiritual condition in an effort to get right with God, who are we really putting in control? Oh, we all know when we fall and fail, and it is right to confess and repent of these shortcomings. But we cannot stop there, for if we do, we are missing out on the full fine-tuning of God's Holy Spirit within us. We must fall to the ground and confess to God that we do not know the depth and despair of our own hearts.

We are truly blind to our own condition. We must cast ourselves upon the rock so He can break us rather than having Him fall down upon us to smash us to pieces. When we cast ourselves willingly upon the rock of our salvation, He will break us, and His Word will pierce us. Yet its ultimate goal is to mend and set our broken bones so they can heal straight. Will we keep walking around on our misshapen perceptions and presumptions, or will we allow the Almighty to shake, to sift, and to refine so we may come forth shining as pure gold? It all starts with laying down what we think we know and understand and truly asking God to search us and seek out the depths of our hearts. Thinking we have arrived only indicates how desperately far we still need to go!

> But Jesus looked at them and said, "What then is this that is written: 'THE STONE WHICH THE BUILDERS REJECTED, THIS BECAME THE CHIEF CORNER stone'? Everyone who falls on that stone will be broken to pieces; but on whomever it falls, it will scatter him like dust." (Luke 20:17–19)

# 60

# He's Got Our Back

> If the Lord is pleased with us, then He will bring us into this land and give it to us–a land which flows with milk and honey. Only do not rebel against the Lord; and do not fear the people of the land, for they will be our prey. Their protection has been removed from them, and the Lord is with us; do not fear them. (Num. 14:8-9)

> For those whom He foreknew, He also predestined to become conformed to the image of His Son, so that He would be the firstborn among many brethren; and these whom He predestined, He also called; and these whom He called, He also justified; and these whom He justified, He also glorified. What then shall we say to these things? If God is for us, who is against us? He who did not spare His own Son, but delivered Him over for us all, how will He not also with Him freely give us all things? (Rom. 8:29-32)

In the middle of the struggle there is more at work than what our eyes see and minds perceive. Indeed, if the Lord is for us who can be against us? There is a level of protection surrounding us that we do not see or comprehend. God is our ever-present help in any trouble. There is constantly a level of spiritual protection surrounding us and fighting on our behalf. We are never alone!

If God is for us then who can be against us? All He calls us to do is go forward in faith. We need to accurately assess the situation before us and seek after wisdom. But beware, God's wisdom at times may run counter to man's natural wisdom and in this there is a critical moment of decision.

Whose wisdom will we choose? The Israelites chose to trust in their natural vision and a bad report. They forgot God's promise and turned from trusting Him. A forty year reprimand resulted. We would be wise to learn from their mistake.

Remember saints, if God is for us who can be against us and prosper? The Almighty is our covering. Run quickly into His arms of love especially when the shadows of uncertainty begin to cloud vision and dampen zeal. Run to Him for strength, direction, and wisdom for the moment. Listen closely for His voice of counsel. Do not doubt even when His wisdom seems to run counter to common sense. In these times snap to attention. When God moves in this way, it may indicate a threshold of a new and wondrous work that He is prepared to birth through the saints' obedience. Do not turn back but run full speed into His arms of love.

If God is for us, who can be against us? Our limited understanding is no match for a powerful and mighty move of God. He hears when we cry with confusion and discouragement. He understands when our faith is feeble and our trust is weak. He knows what obstructive boulders need to be pried out of our spirits to allow us to hear and discern His truth. He desires to unbind our feet and free us to walk with courage and strength. He will clear the path. He will provide the way. He will counsel, encourage, and strengthen with each step. All He asks is that we choose to follow Him and take that first step. It all starts within the confines of our heart. Whose voice will we heed?

Keep listening to the Lord and trust in Him. Our God is for us. No one is stronger or more able than God. Who then shall we fear? There will be times when God calls us forward into a situation that looks destined for defeat. Fear will quickly rise and begin to wrestle for our attention. Uncertainty and confusion will beckon for our devotion. They will rush into any opening we provide through a lack of faith and trust in God. Once admitted into our thought process they will cloud our vision. They invade and mute the receptiveness of our spiritual antennae. We sink into the quicksand of the enemy's lies because we have chosen to tune into fear's insidious intrusion. Praise God, this is not a permanent predicament. All we need do is cry out to Him for deliverance and forgiveness. He loves to hear the voice of His children! Even before we cry He is reaching down to reorient our vision to center on Him. As we respond to the Spirit's nudges we will see that our only hope lies with God. His forgiveness is complete. His tenderness is filled with mercy. His love flows once again through Christ's blood the moment we cry out to Him. How precious is the love of our Father!

Listen once again, if God is for us who can be against us? Let that truth surround your spirit like the unrelenting drum roll summoning the troops to battle. This is war. This war rages for hearts and affections. This war fights over the effectiveness of our mission and efficacy of our prayers. War cries embattle the heart, soul and mind. War-worn saints struggle to bring down the glory of heaven to this battle-weary earth. War. Will we join the battle? Move forward in faith when God calls. Refuse to turn back to old ways and misdirected notions. Rise up and be counted among those who usher in a new move of God! Will we listen, will we follow, and will we obey? If God is for us, who can be against us? Go forward in the power, strength and might of God. Trust in Him. Heed His voice and rise up with a new courage. This is a new day. Let us arise with one heart and choose to glorify our King!

# 61

# Who Sharpens You?

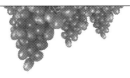

> All things came into being through Him, and apart from Him nothing came into being that has come into being. In Him was life, and the life was the Light of men. The Light shines in the darkness, and the darkness did not comprehend it. (John 1:3–5)

> Iron sharpens iron, so one man sharpens another. (Prov. 27:17)

Bad company corrupts, good company refines. As a man thinketh, so he is. You cannot judge a book by its cover. Still waters run deep. You can tell where a man has walked by the course his life is taking. Are you influencing your world, or is your world influencing you?

These represent many pithy colloquiums with a grain of truth embedded in them. Our past can and will have a huge impact on the way we think and the manner in which we process new experiences and situations. The lenses of our perception are often colored by our former mannerisms, expectations, and experiences. We process things through what we know and have experienced, whether for good or bad. Can we truly break from old habit patterns and thought processes? How do we move into the newness and freshness of what God has for us today, in this hour? Sameness breeds apathy, inattention, and a lack of passion. A fresh wind and the fire of God ignite our imagination and prompt us to dare to dream God's dreams that are only possible with the intervention of the Almighty. When did we begin to settle for things only as broad and deep as we are able to imagine?

The quick and obvious answer is to immerse ourselves in Scripture, but I fear that we often settle for the surface meaning to be found in the Word. We memorize it, we study it, and we quote it, but how often do we sit and truly ponder the wealth and depth of all that Scripture contains? I fear we even approach the Word with the modern world's mentality: a quick fix, a snack, a morsel to see us through. The fast-food drive through approach has even permeated our approach of the Word. Too frequently we consider the quantity of verses read to represent a gourmet meal. There is a good and perfect place for this type of approach of reading the Word, but we cannot stay here as our only type of diet of spiritual food. A broad intake of Scripture is wonderful for giving us the scope of the landscape and acquainting us with the Father's heart and plan for His people and this earth. It gives us a sense of the Father's love and His passion to redeem this fallen earth. It reveals to us the long-awaited Savior and initiates a love dance with our Lord. But if this is the only place we remain, we will never learn any new dance steps!

Our Lord is the master of every dance, and He longs to draw us out and teach us and lead us into new moves! It may be an energetic tango, full of fire and passion that will fill you with the Father's love and desperate longing to know Him and see His love fill this earth. It may be a gentle waltz where He draws you into His arms to nurture and caresses you and carefully lead you through the trials of life. It may be a line dance where He opens your eyes to others who are engaging in their love dance in the same way that He is drawing you. Once He has taught you a particular dance, stretch out it in, embrace it, but do not linger in it when God is calling you to learn some new steps!

Our own personal dance with the Savior will often gravitate toward the ways in which He has gifted us. But there is also a danger that we will plateau and only operate in the level of that gift where we currently reside. Dare to take the Savior's hand and let Him draw you deeper into His heart. He has a new way for you, a deeper knowing of who He is, and a clearer understanding of how completely inadequate we are and how totally awesome and able He is.

It has long filled my imagination about how "Mary treasured all these things in her heart" when she learned from the angel about her privilege to carry the Messiah. (See Luke 2:19.) I fear we have forgotten how to ponder, if we ever knew how in the first place. This takes time, and time seems to the commodity that is the scarcest in our world today.

When God lays a Scripture on your heart, grab hold of it, and like Jacob, refuse to let go until He reveals a fuller and deeper understanding of that portion of the Word. Turn it over again and again in your mind, searching and seeking for the deeper revelation of God to be discovered within. Lean hard into the Spirit, and let Him teach you and guide you through this process. Labor with God, and listen to Him through this process of exploration. Sometimes a clearer understanding of the Word will with come quickly. But you may also find yourself pondering for years over other Scriptures until God brings a deeper truth to your heart. Do not give up. Keep searching and keep seeking, for our God promises that we will find Him when we seek for Him with our whole heart. God began the chase, and He is just beginning to open our eyes and whet our appetite for more and more of Him. Reach up, grab hold of Him, and do not let go until He blesses you!

> I love those who love me; and those who diligently seek me will find me. (Prov. 8:17)

# 62

# Who Is My God?

The LORD your God is with you, He is mighty to save. He will take great delight in you, He will quiet you with his love, He will rejoice over you with singing. (Zeph. 3:17)

Blessed are those who dwell in Your house; they are ever praising You. Blessed are those whose strength is in You, who have set their hearts on a pilgrimage. As they pass through the Valley of Baca, they make it a place of springs; the autumn rains also cover it with pools. They go from strength to strength, till each appears before God in Zion. (Ps. 84:4–7)

Who is this God?

He is my shelter
He is shield
He is my protector
He is my rock
He is my helper
He is my peace
He is my strength
He is my song
He is my redeemer
He is my cleanser
He is my Abba Daddy
He is my counselor
He is my teacher
He is my tear catcher

He is my joy
He leads me beside still waters
He calms my troubled soul
He seeks me
He abides with me
He listens to me—God listens to me!
He pierces all that raises its head between us
He loves me ... He loves me, *He loves me*
He is goodness revealed
He is beauty personified
He is the mighty warrior
He is completely holy
He is mighty
He is faithful
He is true
He is righteous
He is trustworthy
He is and will be victorious
He is the avenger
He is worthy of all honor and glory
He is good
He defines what is good
He is the Creator
He is the Ruler
He is the King of all kings
He is Lord of all lords
He holds the universe in His hands
He raises up and takes down kings
He directs kings' hearts like channels of water
His gaze is loving
His stare is furious

It all depends on the blood

*His love will never die!*

# 63

## How Did My Jesus Die?

The provider of all things good held no earthly possessions.

The one full of knowledge and understanding was fully misunderstood.

The one full of compassion and healing was rejected and hurt.

The demon deliverer was assailed by the demons.

Abducted by soldiers armed for battle, He yielded without protest or fight.

Angelic forces full of God's power and might stood by ready to battle.

The commander of legions never issued the command.

The one who will never leave or desert us was abandoned by His friends.

The faithful one was rejected by the faithless ones.

The light of the dawn was tried in the darkest of night.

The author of justice was tested by the Law misapplied.

The wisdom of heaven was tried by the godless council of man.

The one fully just was unjustly tried.

The merciful healer was wounded, pierced, and whipped without mercy.

The King of kings was stripped of His garments and robes.

The King of the heavens wore man's crown of thorns.

The breaker of sin's chains was bound by chains of iron He created.

Heaven wept while magistrates rejoiced.

Heaven's splendor yielded to man's wrath and scorn.

The Creator was spit upon by His creation.

The all-wise one was ridiculed by the foolish and vain.

The deliverer was delivered up to a crude wooden cross.

The commander of heaven's legions was pierced by a lone solider.

His kingship was used to malign and insult Him.

Pierced with man's nails, He was bound by love to the cross.

Forgiveness reigned amid taunting and jeers.

Sinlessness took on the full depravity of sin.

The one who knew perfect union with the Father endured heaven's silence in agony.

The Creator of the dawn endured the darkest night of the soul.

The provider of wine refused the sponge to deaden pain.

The sustainer and keeper of our souls kept true to His mission.

They sought to take His life, but He willingly gave it.

Healing was delivered as He yielded His life.

The eternal died for the temporal.

One clothed in heaven's glorious splendor was entombed in rags.

They rejoiced as He hung dying; they quaked in fear when He died.

The Creator of the mountains was sealed behind a boulder.

Followers wept while angels encouraged.

Sheer terror was replaced by absolute wonder.

Man's impenetrable seal could not hold God's glory.

He who walked among us has risen above us!

The meekness of the Lamb will come back with the roar of the Lion!

> And in that day I will set about to destroy all the nations that come against Jerusalem. I will pour out on the house of David and on the inhabitants of Jerusalem, the Spirit of grace and of supplication, so that they will look on Me whom they have pierced; and they will mourn for Him, as one mourns for an only son, and they will weep bitterly over Him like the bitter weeping over a firstborn. (Zech. 12:9–10)

> All men are like grass, and all their glory is like the flowers of the field. The grass withers and the flowers fail, because the breath of the Lord blows on them. Surely the people are grass. The grass withers and the flowers fail, but the Word of the Lord stands forever. (Isa. 40:6b–8)

# 64

# Wrestling Match

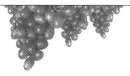

> I find then the principle that evil is present in me, the one who wants to do good. For I joyfully concur with the law of God in the inner man, but I see a different law in the members of my body, waging war against the law of my mind and making me a prisoner of the law of sin which is in my members. Wretched man that I am, who will free me from this body of death? (Rom. 7:21–24)

> And He said to them, "You are those who justify yourselves in the sight of men, but God knows your hearts; for that which is highly esteemed among men is detestable in the sight of God." (Luke 16:15)

The Christian life is not a bed of roses. If we are honest in our pursuit of Christ, we will admit the deeper our faith grows, the more we come to understand how precious little of God's glory we have seen. As our hearts are fine tuned to march with heaven's heartbeat, we become even more aware of the continual battle that wars within our spirits. We are constantly engaged in hand-to-hand combat as we war against the sin that vies for our attention and sets traps for us in every direction.

Praise God for His armor that covers the saints. God's holy covering empowers us, enables us, and protects us as we move forward into the fray. He gives us His peace in the midst of pain and endurance throughout our persecution. We must lean hard into Him in the thick of the struggle. As we depend on God's strength, the battle scars we acquire will radiate with the provision and glory of our King. Daily we battle, and how we handle this warfare deeply influences all those around us and determines how clearly we will shine with the love and victory of Christ.

This grand war of the soul assails us within and without. We wrestle within ourselves as we struggle against the selfish desires that rise up to conflict with the servant attitude pleasing to God. We know what is right and holy before the throne of heaven, but left to our own devices this is often not the path we choose. A telltale sign of this struggle rises whenever we begin to justify our attitudes and actions. Purity and truth need no justification; they will stand on their own merit. So whenever we are rationalizing a plan of action to ourselves, we must pay attention. This is a huge warning flag signaling the battle for our affections is alive and prospering.

We also wrestle among ourselves. If we are not submitting our desires and impulses to the heartbeat of God, we will soon leave the holy imprint of righteousness behind us and begin to emulate the masses around us. The comparison games start, and they will breed nothing but pride and envy. Tongues start wagging, and we begin to fall once again into the trap of elevating ourselves at the expense of others. Gossip raises its ugly head, and our words are no longer used for edification to build up and nurture the body of Christ. This happens so quickly and subtly, and self once again climbs on the throne of our heart. Derogatory words, like a dripping faucet, wear away the unity of the saints. The battle grows thick like a dense fog as the saints battle it out in combat using the weapon of their words.

As if that weren't enough, we also wrestle with the world around us. We know the truth and its power to set us free, but sometimes the road seems too arduous and intense. When the pursuit of ease and self-indulgence of our culture assail our senses, the battle weary will be tempted to throw in the towel and cease struggling against the onslaught of sin. It seems easier to live a life that goes with the flow of culture than to stand up to the immense godlessness that surrounds us. Like chameleons, we blend into our culture instead of standing out and radiating with the glory and beauty of our God. For those who refuse to succumb, the battle often seems unending, with few victories in sight. Even the stout of spirit will be tempted at times to question the effectiveness of their prayers when our society seems to grow darker by the hour. Indeed the conflict between God's standards and the lack of morals in our land grows more pronounced day by day. It would be so easy to give up the fight but for God.

Herein is the rub in our hearts. God has all power and all strength and holds the cosmos in His hands; surely He could intervene at a moment's notice. Yet, He tarries. He has given us one more day to fight in His name, one more day to show grace to our neighbors, and one more day to reach out with the arms of Jesus and offer the hope of life eternal. When we grow weary with the wrestling, we must draw aside and cling to the one who created us. Hold tightly to Him, and declare with Jacob, "I will not let go until You bless me."

Keep holding on, and trust Him to bless you with a deeper love, purer motives, and an overcomer's heart. Only God can take the mess of our hearts and pour into them His perfect provision sufficient to meet the need of every moment. Cling to Him with hope, watch and wait, and you will see the deliverance of your King!

> Then Jacob was left alone, and a man wrestled with him until daybreak. When he saw that he had not prevailed against him, he touched the socket of his thigh; so the socket of Jacob's thigh was dislocated while he wrestled with him. Then he said, "Let me go, for the dawn is breaking." But he said, "I will not let you go unless you bless me." So he said to him, "What is your name?" And he said, "Jacob." He said, "Your name shall no longer be Jacob, but Israel; for you have striven with God and with men and have prevailed." (Gen. 32:24–28)

> Thanks be to God through Jesus Christ our Lord! So then, on the one hand I myself with my mind am serving the law of God, but on the other, with my flesh the law of sin. (Rom. 7:25)

# 65

# Battle Breaker

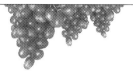

And without faith it is impossible to please God, because anyone who comes to Him must believe that He exists and that He rewards those who earnestly seek Him. (Heb. 11:6)

While Jeremiah was still confined in the courtyard of the guard, the word of the LORD came to him a second time: "This is what the LORD says, He who made the earth, the LORD who formed it and established it—the LORD is His name: 'Call to Me and I will answer you and tell you great and unsearchable things you do not know.'" (Jer. 33:1–2)

Who is this God? He is our leader and the one who breaks through the resistance and lies that assail His holy name. He is the ultimate truth, He is the power above all, and He dwells in the holy of holies. His glory is perfect in its purity, and it cannot be approached by anything unclean or impure. He holds the armies of heaven in His hand, and they snap to attention at any command issuing from His righteous throne. He is the King of glory, and He will share His glory with no other. He is strong and mighty, and He will prevail in battle. He is a warrior King, and He wars for the affections of our hearts. He desires to hear the praises and worship of His people—not because He needs our affirmation but because He knows the benefit awarded our spirits when we willingly align our hearts under His lordship and praise His name. There is healing and power in the name of Jesus. Victory is ours when we follow the Lamb of God. He alone is our strength and our song. He will give us everything pertaining to goodness and godliness. So how do we find Him in the midst of the battle when we have grown weary and disheartened?

Jeremiah gives us a valuable clue as to arming ourselves in the crux of the battle. Even while confined in the courtyard of the guard, God's Word still spoke to him and encouraged him. Walls could not bar God from meeting the need of his servant! God, in His mercy and love, reminded Jeremiah of His power and authority to call his spirit to attention. This was almighty God speaking, so sit up and take notice! A reminder of Jehovah's ownership of all the earth would give Jeremiah the confidence to fully trust God to deliver on His promises. God calls Jeremiah to engage with Him, and He prompts Jeremiah to pray for wisdom and understanding. This was the second time God spoke to Jeremiah. Surely God knew the need Jeremiah had to be encouraged and fortified, and He met Jeremiah right at his point of need. Yet God went beyond the basic needs of the moment and promised Jeremiah even greater treasures than just physical freedom. He promises him wondrous truths and revelations and an opening to the wonders of heaven, if Jeremiah would but ask.

This implies that even in the midst of the battle, if you will lean into Him and trust in His character, God will meet you right where you are, even if you don't get it the first time! He will deliver you from your limited understanding, for it is His nature to bless His people. It is His desire to draw you even deeper into His heart of love. There is no way to exhaust the resources and power of our God and King! All He asks is that you call to Him and trust in the character of His nature and the exquisiteness of His timing to deliver precisely what you need at exactly the right moment. He has so much more to give if you will seek His face and approach Him with a steadfast faith. God is calling. God is drawing you to Himself that He might reveal more of His wonder and glory to the world-weary heart.

When God reaches down to touch in an unexpected way, do you embrace the beauty of a new depth of revelation, or do you turn away because it rattles your comfort zone? When God is poised to bless and honor you for *His* name's sake, do you reject His favor with a sense of false humility—"I am not worth it"? Of course you are worth His blessing! You were bought with a price, and you are a child of the King of kings! Or (and this is equally as dangerous) do you demand honor? Remember, pride goes before the fall. It is a precarious balancing act to walk the line between true humility and righteous, holy expectation and not fall into the trap of presuming on God or succumbing to pride. Truly no one can do this in him or herself; only the Spirit of God working within the heart can give you this godly balance in your spirit!

Are you willing to throw everything you have in with God even when you don't understand where or how He is leading you? If you demand understanding in everything, who is really on the throne of your heart? There are seasons when God calls you to wrestle with Him. He draws you to cling to Him and fervently seek His face and His favor. Is it presumptuous to desperately cry out for God's blessing? Not if you have the spirit of a Jeremiah and the heart of one who is willing to reach up to God for those great and mighty things you do not know. When God moves to answer this earnest heart plea, you will find that although it is wondrous, it will also leave you hungry for more. More of God's presence, passion, and pleasure will become your heart's pursuit. A journey of seeking after God's own heart has been birthed, and it will be a lifelong journey. Heavenly wrestling has finally begun, and nothing will satisfy other than seeing a purer and deeper revelation of God. With each new step and each fresh revelation, your desire for His presence will grow deeper, more intense, increasingly poignant, and precisely focused. The lure of earth will begin to fade away as your heart learns to hunger for the glories of heaven to be poured forth into weary hearts and upon a war-ravaged land. Let the battle begin!

> You will seek me and find me when you seek me with all your heart. I will be found by you," declares the LORD, "and will bring you back from captivity!" (Jer. 29:13–14)

# 66

## Worry or Worship

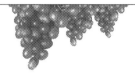

I will bless the LORD at all times; His praise shall continually be in my mouth. My soul will make its boast in the LORD; the humble will hear it and rejoice. O magnify the LORD with me, and let us exalt His name together. I sought the LORD, and He answered me, and delivered me from all my fears. … The angel of the LORD encamps around those who fear Him, and rescues them. O taste and see that the LORD is good; how blessed is the man who takes refuge in Him! … The eyes of the LORD are toward the righteous and His ears are open to their cry. … The righteous cry, and the LORD hears and delivers them out of all their troubles. The LORD is near to the brokenhearted and saves those who are crushed in spirit. Many are the afflictions of the righteous, but the LORD delivers him out of them all. (Ps. 34:1–4, 7–8, 15, 17–19)

Worry—we all know this emotion all too well. It pervades our culture and is constantly present, ready to assail our minds. What do we do with it? We know God promises to meet us in every need and situation, but how do we handle our emotions when our circumstances again challenge our level of trust in the Lord? As I contemplated my innate reactions to times of stress, God bent down low to speak to my heart. He comforted, challenged, exhorted, and encouraged. These intimate moments with the Savior revealed His wonderful, kind, and gentle heart of love. Listen in to His gentle admonition:

> When the worry bug tries to bite, there are two basic responses. You can embrace it and dance with it or hold it at arm's length with the vehicle of praise. Your reflex response is to entertain it, turn it over, and try to look at it from all angles. Your mind tells you to dig in and worry, pray, worry, pray, worry, pray,

worry. But this is merely the starting gate. This progression marks a heart that is turning to Me and trying to yield the worry bug completely over to Me. It is a good place to be but not the best …

If you desire to grow in worship, you must move on to the next step. When the situation is beyond your control (truly, is any situation really in your control? Can you hear God's gentle laugh here?), you must start by worshipping what you know to be true: My character and My revealed truths in Scripture.

Worship Me, especially when you do not understand where I am going or how I am moving. Worship Me for what I have already shown you. Go back to those stones of remembrance in your walk with Me, and worship Me for My faithfulness there. Then move in faith to worship Me in areas where you don't understand, areas of doubt, uncertainty, and even disbelief. Praise Me. Remember that I am bigger than your area of unbelief and that I can draw you through discouragement into a deeper and bigger understanding of who I am.

Worship Me for who I am, not for just what I am doing.

In this present situation, you have no idea where I am going or when and how I will intervene. Stand in your faith and praise Me. List My characteristics back to Me in praise and worship and you will begin to view things with the lens of heaven. Your faith will be stretched, and your confidence and trust in Me will grow. My attributes do not change, but as you praise Me in those attributes, your understanding of the depth and purity of My love will grow by leaps and bounds. This can happen no other way. Remember, I inhabit the praise of My people. It is your greatest weapon; your enemy cannot stand to hear My praises ascending into the courtrooms of heaven. It is sweet incense, and it purifies the depths of your soul. So come to Me, worship with empty hands, and I will fill your heart to overflowing. Joy will be yours, and it will be with such a depth of purity and intensity that the world cannot snatch it away. Refuse to worry and rejoice, for it is healing to the bones and sustains the weary heart. Come, My child, rejoice!

—Love, Abba

# 67

# The Rock

Trust in the LORD forever, for in God the LORD, we have an everlasting the Rock. (Isa. 26:4)

You do not change. You are the same yesterday, today, and forever. You are the Rock that does not move, the Rock that no storm can diminish, and the Rock that stands firm throughout the generations of time. When I focus on that Rock, I am secure, I am sheltered, and I am steady. When my gaze is diverted, my vision of the Rock dims, as if I am looking at it with the beginning of cataracts. The film covering my eyes is the concern of this world. How quickly the world's view discolors my perceptions, and how swiftly my affections can be realigned to conform with those of the society about me—all because I took my eyes off of the Rock. When did my gaze falter? Am I looking at the Lord as my lover or my judge?

The longer we gaze into His beautiful countenance, the more we see and understand the purity of His love. We come to long after the cleansing fire His love initiates and hunger for a deeper intimacy with Him. Make no mistake: as you focus on the Rock, it will not be for platitudes and comfort but for a cleansing so deep, so purifying that you will wonder how you ever could have been content with your former state. Will we allow Him to search us and seek us; will we open ourselves up to the searing, loving gaze of our Lord? Will we indeed count it as all joy, knowing Him even when the refining process brings pain?

Keep looking to the Rock. Though forces swirl about your feet, beckoning you to break eye contact, keep focused. Remember His deeds of old. Recount His faithfulness throughout Scripture and to you personally. Our

God does not fail. Remember and keep repeating the memories of His faithfulness no matter how hot and fierce the battle gets.

Our God, the eternal one, dwells in us. Can you fathom the depth and wonder of it all? God is with us. Immanuel. God is in us—the wonder of Pentecost! What more could anyone need? He has sealed our future through His sacrifice on the cross, and He has empowered us to live victoriously in this life through His Holy Spirit. There is nowhere we can escape His love.

He is reaching out.

Are you reaching up? Will you remain engaged no matter how hot and purifying His fire grows within your soul? Woe to those who turn away. The journey's end is in sight. Keep your eyes focused on the goal, and remember nothing—no, nothing, no matter how deep the pain, dark the night, or fierce the storm—can separate you from His love. Will you welcome His fire when it falls, and will you let it do its cleansing?

> "Answer me, O LORD, answer me, that this people may know that You, O LORD, are God, and that You have turned their heart back again." Then the fire of the LORD fell and consumed the burnt offering and the wood and the stones and the dust, and licked up the water that was in the trench. When all the people saw it, they fell on their faces; and they said, "The LORD, He is God; the LORD, He is God." (1 Kings 18:37–39)

# 68

# Purpose behind the Pain

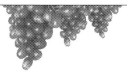

> Whoever speaks, is to do so as one who is speaking the utterances of God; whoever serves is to do so as one who is serving by the strength which God supplies; so that in all things God may be glorified through Jesus Christ, to whom belongs the glory and dominion forever and ever. Amen. Beloved, do not be surprised at the fiery ordeal among you, which comes upon you for your testing, as though some strange thing were happening to you; but to the degree that you share the sufferings of Christ, keep on rejoicing, so that also at the revelation of His glory you may rejoice with exultation. (1 Peter 4:11–13)

The Christ-centered life is one that rejoices in the opportunity and pleasure of serving the King. We put our hand to the plow and joyously look forward to the huge fields that God has for us to plow with His hand guiding ours. When we consider all the possibilities for the glory of the kingdom to flow down through our obedience, it is almost easy to become giddy with pleasure and a divine joy. One victorious step forward and it appears that the rewards of heaven are just within our grasp. Once we have seen a snippet of God's glorious provision, it becomes crystal clear that this is exactly what we were created for—to walk in unison with the Holy Spirit and rejoice in the God of our salvation.

It would appear that nothing can stop us, for God is on our side! When we use the weapon of His Word and secret laser beam of intercessory prayer, it would appear that we can take down any fortress and that truly nothing is outside of the miraculous touch of an Almighty God! A major spiritual victory brings incredible, joyous dancing in the streets of our soul. God has shown up again and slain the onslaught of His foes. We are His, and He is ours. Hallelujah! In the middle of the rejoicing, a sweet and quiet awe begins to grow within our soul. Truly our God is wondrous and exalted. Why would we run to another?

Yet, when the routine of our daily lives begins to filter back in, this awe begins to subside. In this moment, the enemy can catch us unaware and cause us to trip and hurl headlong into doubt and despair if we are not careful. It is often within the greatest victory the swiftest piercing test comes. How will we handle the times when we have beheld the glory and majesty of God intervening on our behalf? In our instant-gratification type of society, it is so easy to fall into the trap of believing that once we have seen the provision of God it will be smooth sailing, as if we had finally crested the mountaintop of our spiritual climb. But within the time of our victory dance, God has a gentle way of refining and purifying us yet further. He will bring to us naysayers, doubters, and even insincere flatterers; and they are the worst of all. If we fall into the lure of their flowing words of exaltation, we are in danger of gathering the glory to ourselves and not reflecting it back to its rightful owner—God. When we become glory grabbers, we are in essence stealing from God Himself!

In the times of our victory afterglow, we must remain sensitive to the Spirit's leading and gentle nudging. For if not, we will become victim to the next trap the enemy has laid for us. Trials and testing will continue to come, and if we are not careful, it is easy to begin to shake our fists to heaven and declare God callous for not protecting us and providing for us smooth sailing because we have obeyed and overcome. How earth bound is our vision and appetite! If we could only see with God's eyes, we would behold how each misstep and challenge is just a training tool in the Master's hand. When we taste a sampling of His glory, there is always more and a fuller course to experience; and that often happens through the experience of the pitfalls we find riding on the coattails of our glorious spiritual victories.

When we are in the trenches of warfare, we come to see that God truly does have our back. He is leading the advance party of righteousness into the deepest part of our soul and weeding out all that is contrary to the beauty and totality of His goodness. He does salt us with fire so we may become even saltier and more effective in this war between the kingdom of heaven and the prince of this world. Rejecting the fire of His training will render us ineffective and prohibit us from tasting a further experience of His glory that flows in the midst of the battle. In our flesh, we continually hunger for the solution and praise party that comes following the conclusion of our struggles. Yet it is in the very midst of the battle that God is creating within us a degree of saltiness that will preserve an entire generation. Are we willing to endure the heat of the test so we may reach more, save more, and lead the way home to a lost and deeply broken people? Our answer will highlight whose glory we are truly seeking.

> These things I have spoken to you, so that in Me you may have peace. In the world you have tribulation, but take courage; I have overcome the world. (John 16:33)

> For everyone will be salted with fire. Salt is good; but if the salt becomes unsalty, with what will you make it salty again? Have salt in yourselves, and be at peace with one another. (Mark 9:49–50)

# 69

## Mourning Song

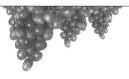

Oh Lord, please come to me
And give me understanding
The young die soon
The old linger on
Oh who's to understand
The movement of Your hand?
Do Your mercies still stand?

The grief burns deep
The tears fall down
I bear unbearable pain
Your hand is there
It won't let go
But bids me peace in sorrow
Hold on until tomorrow

I look around
Up and down
Inside and out
If I could change this
Or alter that
Would it be the same
Or could things have been
    changed?

But what is the use in that
My weary soul cries
What can come
Of all the pain
I am not satisfied
My heart's empty inside

From dawn to dusk
From dusk to dawn
The pain lingers on
It draws me in
Surrounds my soul
My loved one is still gone
How can I carry on?

"Look up and out"
I hear Your cry
You're always by my side
You understand,
You've felt it all
When Your precious Son died
It was for me He died

He holds me closely
To His side
So I can hear Him say,
"Child, give Me all your pain
It's too big for you to hold
It wearies body and soul
And quickly makes you old

"I offer peace
Strength, and joy
If you will yield to Me
All your questions
And your pain
They need not remain
But will be exchanged

"For a deep, profound peace
That man cannot understand"
A great exchange
How can it be?
My Savior suffers for me
His love sets me free
He truly liberates me

So now I sing
Of His great love
That never lets go
It holds me close
Through good and bad
So how can I be sad?
Sorrow is gone, I'm so glad!

# 70

# Shelter of the Most High

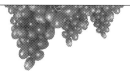

> He who dwells in the shelter of the Most High will abide in the shadow of the Almighty. I will say to the LORD, "My refuge and my fortress, My God, in whom I trust!" For it is He who delivers you from the snare of the trapper and from the deadly pestilence. (Ps. 91:1–3)

*What does it mean to abide in the shelter of the Most High?*

It means to not lean on our own understanding.

It means to not treat Him as the last resort.

It means being willing to totally entrust God for others who you want to know God's glory.

It means pushing forward in your faith walk, even when it may mean leaving others behind who don't share in your same level of passion for Jesus. (At first this may seem brutal, until you remember that their growth and maturity also lies with your Lord.)

It means to stop trying to orchestrate the lives of others but giving them the freedom to reach up and pursue God according to the way the Holy Spirit draws them.

It means to seek Him first, above all things, in all things, and in spite of all things.

It means to stand and watch—watch for His salvation and His provision.

It means declaring the promises and provisions of the King, even when you don't see them (Abraham).

It means accepting His manna rather than the seven-course gourmet meals of the world.

It means abiding in His peace and power, accepting what you cannot change, and bringing those things to the throne of grace.

It means choosing not to fear but to lean hard into His Word, clinging to it as if your life depended on it.

It means to pursue God without looking back and longing for the leisure and pleasures of days gone by.

It means to hunger after God with a thirst so powerful nothing else will satisfy.

It means you are willing to stop trying to fix things on your own.

It means you are willing to sit at His feet, bringing your praise and petitions to Him, and wait for His instruction.

It means you have a heart that is willing to abide in the wilderness with Jesus rather than in the comfort and fleeting pleasures of the world.

It means you will allow Him to woo you and love you and that you will sit in His presence.

It is knowing that even in the darkness, God is there.

It is in the remembering that He will never leave nor forsake you.

It means accepting, even welcoming, the pruning of your spirit.

It means accepting His perfect peace and not stubbornly returning to the "what ifs?"

It means being willing to lay down all your questions at His feet.

It means praising Him for who He is, even when there is turmoil swirling about.

It means praising Him for His provision, even before you have seen it delivered.

It means being willing to live as a marked man, set apart for the purpose and pleasure of the King!

It means your heart and affections stay with God even in the thickest battle.

It is aligning with Job to say "Yea, even though He slay me, I will trust in Him."

It means clinging to God because you know all flesh is but grass and only God will endure.

It means you have a peace, a rest, and a steadfastness about you that the world cannot understand.

It all comes down to a simple trust and faith in Jesus.

Will you lean hard into Him and lean not on your own understanding?

# 71

# The Thoughts Have It

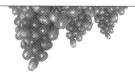

Let no man deceive himself. If any man among you thinks that he is wise in this age, he must become foolish, so that he may become wise. For the wisdom of this world is foolishness before God. For it is written, "He is THE ONE WHO CATCHES THE WISE IN THEIR CRAFTINESS"; and again, "THE LORD KNOWS THE REASONINGS of the wise, THAT THEY ARE USELESS." So then let no one boast in men. (1 Cor. 3:18–21)

According to the grace of God which was given to me, like a wise master builder I laid a foundation, and another is building on it. But each man must be careful how he builds on it. For no man can lay a foundation other than the one which is laid, which is Jesus Christ. (1 Cor. 3:10–11)

Seek the LORD while He may be found; call upon Him while He is near. Let the wicked forsake his way and the unrighteous man his thoughts; and let him return to the LORD, and He will have compassion on him, and to our God, for He will abundantly pardon. (Isa. 55:6–7)

What do we truly love—the applause and approval of men or the wisdom and counsel of God? The place we most often stumble and fall is in our thought life, for as a man thinketh, so he is. (See Prov. 23:7.) What is feeding our thoughts? Whose voice percolates through our minds? Have we truly brought every thought into submission and obedience to Christ?

As we continue on in our pursuit of the Christian life, we are prone to judge our journey by our actions and accomplishments. Yet, anything we are able to achieve has been first wrought by the hand of God. He draws us to our position and equips us for our area of influence. He has given us every talent we possess to fulfill our good works. Why would we dare to take the credit?

It is only when we realize how desperately needy we are that we finally are willing to cast every hope, dream, and aspiration into the arms of our God and trust Him with the fulfillment of who He has called us to become. Where are you being poured out as a drink offering unto the glory of God? This is your life's greatest calling, and it is from the platform of utter brokenness that God performs His greatest work. It is in the season of interrupted dreams that God shifts, sifts, and sorts our character. It is when we have nothing left to give, and when we reach up and cry out with abandon to the Maker of our souls, that God loves to bend down in compassion. As we yield to His touch, He blows on the embers of hope residing in our soul and ignites a holy passion that burns with a clarity and focus that was only before a mere shadow of His glory. Where self had reigned, the depth and power of His radiance was veiled. As self is laid aside, the fullness of almighty God begins to shine and radiate through our spirits. So let's rejoice in our brokenness and shout, "Glory, God reigns!" His purposes will be accomplished. He is willing to draw us through a season of delayed hope and impoverished dreams to refine our focus and point us back toward Him.

Jesus is all we need. Is Jesus our heart's desire? Will we take the risk to lay our hopes at His feet and plead with Him to impart the passions of His heart into these very human frames? How different we would be if we were completely aligned with the heart of God! Yet in His mercy, God continues to refine and purify and test us—our actions, our motives, and our thoughts. He knows it all, and He calls us back to align our hearts and spirits with His passions. So where has your mind been dwelling? Our thoughts are a mere reflection of where we choose to camp with our spirits. The focus and fruit of our lives will in turn be largely impacted by how we think. What or who shapes your thought life? Is it the truth found in Christ Jesus, our cornerstone? Any other foundation will crumble and fall. Only the attitudes and works built on the truth revealed through Christ will stand and endure.

Lord, draw us back to build on Jesus, and unify our hearts to bring Him glory, honor, and praise in all things. May everything in us shout, "Glory, hallelujah, our God reigns!" Amen.

# 72

# Weight of Glory

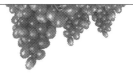

> Therefore we do not lose heart, but though our outer man is decaying, yet our inner man is being renewed day by day. For momentary, light affliction is producing for us an eternal weight of glory far beyond all comparison, while we look not at the things which are seen, but at the things which are not seen; for the things which are seen are temporal, but the things which are not seen are eternal. (2 Cor. 4:16–18)

> The soul of the sluggard craves and gets nothing, but the soul of the diligent is made fat. (Prov. 13:4)

The beauty of the Christian walk is that it is uniquely intimate and personal. The Maker of our souls loves us, and He knows us full well. He knows every hope and dream. He sees how they intermingle to shape the course of our life's journey. He knows where our failures hamstring our progress in the faith and dampen the zeal of our spirits. He sees how we sow seeds of righteousness and when we fall prey once again to the temptations that ever clamor for our attention.

Praise God for the blood of Christ that has cleansed us from all our sin! Sin's penalty has been taken by Jesus, and we are free from the fear of punishment. Christ has borne God's wrath for us, so the Father no longer sees our sin stain. While the fear of punishment is absolved, there are still resident memories that color our hope. The recollection of each misstep and every misfortune is held lovingly in our Father's hands. They are being woven carefully together to create within us a heart of beauty that reflects the glory of the King. He uses every exploit and all of our memories to gently shape and craft within us the beautiful glory of Jesus Himself. Nothing is wasted. Nothing is useless. Nothing is vain, as long as it all has been yielded up for the Master's use to refine and purify our spirits.

God reaches down, and we are changed from glory to glory. With just one masterful touch, the memory is healed. Earth's view is eclipsed by the perspective of heaven, and we are forever changed. Gone is the shame, the despair and hopelessness. The sting of our sin is completely washed away as we see how God was moving. In faithfulness He uses even our greatest weakness as a touch point to pour into our spirits the fullness of His glory. Where others see utter weakness and foolishness, God sees potential and a portal for the eternal to pour forth. All He asks of us is a yielded heart and open hands.

As we once again lay all of our burdens at His feet, we are renewed, refreshed, and refueled. As we run hard after God, we will find that everything in us begins to conform to the likeness of Jesus. Our soul is made fat with the weight of the glory of heaven. There is no other way to attain to this fullness of spirit other than wrestling with God and holding on until the glory of the Almighty breaks through the mists that surround our souls. The most battle-worn saint will have seen glimpses of glory that the casual observer can only dream about. Will we turn to welcome the pursuer of our hearts?

Our Father admonishes us to take captive every thought to the obedience of Christ. The frontline of the battle is in the minefield of our thoughts. The aim of our thoughts will either serve self or honor God. Left to ourselves, self will ever raise its ugly head and claim the predominance. It is here that sin is conceived and begins to pulsate with desire. The Lord searches us throughout. He knows all of our thoughts, our intentions, and the deepest corners of our hearts. He sees it all, and yet He still loves us, He still woos us, and He still promises to never, ever leave or desert us. Will we set aside all that clamors for our attention and draw near to God to sit at His feet? It is an awesome concept. This morsel of dust reaches up toward the throne room of heaven. God sees, God smiles, and He reaches down through all the muck and worry of this world to comfort, console, edify, exhort, and equip. We will find, as we continue to pursue the righteousness of God, that we have been immeasurably changed. The glory of heaven will cover our spirits, and we will carry about us the aroma of Jesus wherever we go. May your soul grow ever fatter with the fullness of God's love!

# 73

# Abram, Man of God

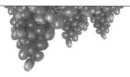

Now when the sun was going down, a deep sleep fell upon
Abram; and behold, *terror and great darkness fell upon him.*
God said to Abram, "Know for certain that your descendants
will be strangers in a land that is not theirs, where they will
be enslaved and oppressed four hundred years. But I will also
judge the nation whom they will serve, and afterward they
will come out with many possessions. As for you, you shall go
to your fathers in peace; you will be buried at a good old age."
(Gen. 15:12–15, emphasis added)

Abram, the one to whom God showed such favor and blessing, was also
shown the horror of the coming exile of Israel as slaves to Egypt. He would
carry this burden in his spirit the rest of his earth-bound days. Yet, even as
he walked in the knowledge of what was to come, God's glory came down
and consumed his offering. (See Gen. 15:17.) It was pleasing in God's sight
that Abram yielded his physical being and his spirit to the Lord almighty.
In the physical he offered what he had upon the altar of sacrifice. In his
spirit, he groaned with the knowledge of what would become of God's
people. Yet even with this knowledge, he did not turn away from God but
rather turned toward Him and continued to walk in faithfulness with his
offering. (Read all of Gen.15.) Truly God was growing a leader to align
him after God's heart and passions.

Prior to this night terror, Abram had just received the promise of a blessing
to ease his aching heart. Childless, he had begun to lose hope for an heir.
God brought him to the point of an almost-abandoned dream before
intervening to renew His promise to Abram for his descendants. How
Abram's heart must have rejoiced at this news. Surely God saw his need

and his heart's desire for progeny. God met him at his point of need and bowed down low with a magnificent promise: descendants as numerous as the stars (v. 5)! To ratify this covenant, God prompted Abram to bring forward an offering. Yet before the offering was consumed, Abram fell into a deep sleep. Joy was turned to terror as he was shown the future of his promised descendants. How his heart must have ached. He had fought the battle of faith to remain steadfastly focused on God's promise in spite of the delayed fulfillment. Finally, he was secure in God's promise. Life looked complete. His rejoicing was full, until sleep fell at twilight.

God showed Abram the horrors his descendants would face in their captivity. Yet God did not leave him in agony. He also promised judgment to the oppressors once the time of exile had been fulfilled. The purging complete, God would once again free His people. As Abram assimilated the raw truth of this night vision, God bent down low and comforted his heart with the promise of a long life and personal peace. Can you hear Abram's heartbeat? "I am blessed, but future generations will be slaves. Who can understand such a thing? Oh, that God would prevent this horror. Be at rest, my soul, trust God. He will surely deliver them just as He has met me here today. God is faithful."

This illustrates the spiritual tension we experience as we look forward to being one day reunited with our Lord Jesus. For now we walk in a world filled with sin. We are all too aware of sorrows that afflict the righteous and the judgment to come for those who do not turn to Jesus. How can it be that at the same time the troubles of the world weigh on our spirits that we can rejoice in and praise God for the abundance of His blessings? To the world we must look like we are schizophrenic as we rejoice even in the midst of deep suffering and trial. Only by the grace of God can we find where true peace lies: in the loving arms of our Savior, who will never let us go! Rest in Him, dear one, knowing He who holds your future is securely holding you now! Willingly join in the sufferings of Christ now, knowing that as you do, far greater riches are being stored up in heaven for you. Hold onto the hope that does not disappoint. Righteousness will triumph, and we will see victory in the arms of our Savior.

# 74

# The Approach

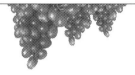

"Come now, and let us reason together," Says the LORD, "Though your sins are as scarlet, they will be as white as snow; though they are red like crimson, they will be like wool. If you consent and obey, you will eat the best of the land; But if you refuse and rebel, you will be devoured by the sword." Truly, the mouth of the LORD has spoken. (Isa. 1:18–20)

And I pray that the fellowship of your faith may become effective through the knowledge of every good thing which is in you for Christ's sake. (Philem. 1:6)

God is good, all the time. His mercy endures throughout the generations. He has always been and will always be. He is the same yesterday, today, and tomorrow. He is the ultimate in consistency, and He is the definition of faithfulness. His words stand, and He says what He means. He is absolute, almighty, incorruptible, and completely powerful. He is clothed in mercy and grace toward His children, and He tells us to come. Come to Him, all who are weary and heavy laden, and He will indeed give you rest. (See Matt. 11:28.) Come with your broken heart, your weary feet, and your shattered dreams. Come be refueled, refreshed, and renewed. Come.

He calls and He waits. He seeks and He searches. He reaches out and longs for His creation to turn once again to Him. He is calling, ever calling, come. But how do we come? It is imperative to approach the throne of grace with an attitude pleasing in the courts of heaven. God reminds us who we are; clean, pure, and holy because of the blood. His words indeed act as a two-edged sword. For the downtrodden, discouraged, and defeated, He reminds us that He has already done the work of refining and purifying us through the blood of Christ. To the proud and arrogant, He firmly reminds us of our helpless state to redeem and cleanse ourselves. In all things, He is always pointing us toward the cross of mercy and grace.

He is calling, "Come, have no fear. You are accepted, loved, and forgiven."

Can you hear Him calling, "I hold out my arms for you. How I long to gather you into My arms of love to be your shelter and friend. But you were unwilling."?

When we run to Him in our brokenness, He stretches out His compassion and boundless love to envelop us, pick us up, mend our hearts, and set us back on our feet. Then He tells us to go out and run the race with endurance once again, continually looking to Him as our coach to guide and direct our steps. The devastated one who has been lifted from the garbage heap and healed through God's incredible mercy will long remember the goodness of God. His worship will be purer and more profound because of the pathway he has walked. He truly has learned what it is to worship from a position of desperate need. As long as he walks forward with his reliance centered and focused on God, there will be nothing that can impede the extent of his testimony's power. Even in a healed state, God is still calling us to always come, moment by moment, incident by incident, experience after experience, come.

When we refuse to draw aside and come to God, we begin once again to sink into the quicksand of self-delusion. Having overcome, there is a subtle snare waiting to worm its way into our hearts, whispering to us seductive flattery. It brings forth partial evidence, which warps our memory with selective scenes of our success. When these thoughts go unchecked, we will rapidly spiral in a downward direction as we begin to garner praise and credit unto our own account and ignore the mercy of God. We become glory grabbers, and heaven looks on, incredulous, and weeps again over the sway of sin. Yet even here, God is calling, "Come, let us reason together."

If we will listen to the nudges of the Spirit and willingly put the brakes on the roller coaster of self-promotion, we will hear the strong admonition of God. Reason with Him and remember. Remember where He first found you. Remember how He picked you up when there was no good or grace to be found in your spirit. Remember how He whispered to your soul to draw you to the cross. Remember the depth and depravity of your sin. Remember the cross. Remember. Weep and rejoice for the incredible and matchless grace God has given and the glorious awful price He paid to win you back. Remember, fall on your face with hands lifted high and exalt Him with everything you have.

He has deposited all that Christ has to offer into the fragile vessel of man. He has cleansed us and filled us with a heavenly deposit that is rich and full of glory. Again, He calls us to come. Saints, we must pick up God's sword and enter into the fray. God has provided all we need for goodness and godliness. We have been given heaven's incredible treasure poured into our earthly vessels. Let us continue to press in further to God's heart and willingly pour out all we have as a thank offering unto His feet. As we come to adore and reverence, as we draw aside to wrestle and reason with God, He will cleanse away the impurities that bind our feet. He will equip us with a clearer vision and straighten out the direction of our intent. He will once again set us upon the high and holy walk He has uniquely designed for each one. Come, reason with God, and be restored, renewed, and refocused. God holds out His hands for you. He is calling. It is time to come.

# 75

# Command of the Lord

> "Though Balak were to give me his house full of silver and gold, I could not do anything contrary to the command of the Lord, either good or bad, of my own accord. What the Lord speaks, that I will speak"? … He took up his discourse and said, "The oracle of Balaam the son of Beor, and the oracle of the man whose eye is opened, the oracle of him who hears the words of God, and knows the knowledge of the Most High, who sees the vision of the Almighty, falling down, yet having his eyes uncovered. I see him, but not now; I behold him, but not near; a star shall come forth from Jacob, a scepter shall rise from Israel, and shall crush through the forehead of Moab, and tear down all the sons of Sheth. Edom shall be a possession, Seir, its enemies, also will be a possession, while Israel performs valiantly. (Num. 24:13, 15–18)

As Balaam spoke the Holy Spirit–inspired words of God, it is doubtful that King Balak discerned the depth of their revelation. God was speaking His heart to redeem and prosper His people in the midst of her enemies. He already had the victory planned in the matchless worth of Jesus' sacrifice. He was committed to guide and lead His people toward the fullness of His salvation and wonder of His grace. Yet Balak had no comprehension of the passion of God for His people or the sureness of their deliverance.

So too, we walk among a people who have been rendered spiritually deaf by the lies of the enemy. Although we speak of the glory of heaven to come, few have ears to hear. The worries and troubles of this world fully consume their attention. They have been deluded to think that they are masters of their own destiny and so they run a race doomed to futility from the start. Tuned into the lie that just a little more effort or one lucky break will be their turning point, they keep running after false promises swirling in gusts of wind.

Jesus looks with compassion on these creatures without a shepherd. We also must focus on the heart of God and reach out in love. He calls us to dedicate ourselves to speaking His words in integrity and truth. We must declare with Balaam that no matter the cost or loss of honor, we will speak the words God has given. We bring Him no joy when we shrink back in self-conscious fear or timidity. He is still calling to His people, "Be strong and courageous!" Will you hear the call?

There is a prize set before us. If we will learn to view everything through the perspective of Jesus' imminent return, our passions will align more closely with our Lord's heartbeat. Let us all look forward with joy and eagerness to His second coming. If we truly know Him and have experienced the depth of His love, this will hold no fear but a deepening anticipation and hunger for Him. A desperate need for God must burn with an unquenchable fire in our spirits. Only this type of passion will keep us focused on the narrow path. It will guard us from fear; it will order our steps and continually tweak our affections.

Let the Lord go on a "seek and search" mission in your spirit. Invite Him to sift through all the depths of your affections and pain-filled memories. Let Him renew you from within. As His fire begins to filter into your heart, lift your hands in wonder and amazement. Honor Him with every breath, and cling to Him as if your every moment was dependent on His grace. Reality check—it does!

Press into God and pour your passions before His feet. Seek after His heart, and hunger for opened eyes and cleared ears. Pleas for godly discernment will be met in the gracious arms of a loving Father. Don't miss these depths of God's passions because you would not ask.

# 76

# Guide Me

Guide me and lead me and heal me, oh Lord,
That I would follow Your ways.
Guide me and lead me and heal me, oh Lord,
To honor You all my days.
Your ways are higher than my thoughts,
Your counsel is pure and sweet.
It guides and leads and instructs me,
And gently directs my feet.

Guide me and lead me and heal me, oh Lord,
That I might worship You all my days.
Guide me and lead me and heal me, oh Lord,
To gladly offer You my praise.
Praise rises sweet as incense,
Heaven's songs descend night and day.
They shout and ring with your glory,
They're not silent and prompt me to obey.

Guide me and lead me and heal me, oh Lord,
And center me on Your way.
Guide me and lead me and heal me, oh Lord,
And cover me and help me stay,
Close to Your heart so tender,
Yet firm, steadfast, and sure.
You counsel and instruct me,
To make my ways increasingly pure.

Guide me and lead me and heal me, oh Lord,
And lead me swiftly home.
Guide me and lead me and heal me, oh Lord,
And help me to no longer roam,
From your Word and its counsel.
It is tried, faithful, and true.
It will not return unfruitful,
But will gently my spirit renew.

Guide me and lead me and heal me, oh Lord,
Help the fire to not grow dim.
Guide me and lead me and heal me, oh Lord,
Burn Your love brightly within.
Open my eyes to see more clearly,
Draw me closer to Your side.
Cast off all my doubt and fear,
Let my heart in You abide.

Guide me and lead me and heal me, oh Lord,
And I will lead others in the way.
Guide me and lead me and heal me, oh Lord,
To offer the comfort that will stay.
For You have shown me goodness,
Each day I've walked this earth.
You've covered me and guided me,
Each day since my birth.

Guide me and lead me and heal me, oh Lord,
As long as You give me breath.
Guide me and lead me and heal me, oh Lord,
Every moment until my death.
For on that sweet, glorious day,
Your grace will usher me home.
Your face I will finally see,
All done are the days I did roam.

Guide me and lead me and heal me, oh Lord,
To stay close by Your side.
Guide me and lead me and heal me, oh Lord,
And be my forever guide.
I do not have the wisdom,
Or strength of mighty men.
But you have given unto me,
The impact and power of the pen!

Guide me and lead me and heal me, oh Lord,
To remember it's all from You.
Guide me and lead me and heal me, oh Lord,
For only then can I be true.
To the call you have gently placed,
So deeply within my heart.
It's led and covered me all of my days,
Right from the moment of my start.

Guide me and lead me and heal me, oh Lord,
Though I don't know the full plan.
Guide me and lead me and heal me, oh Lord,
And remind me that You understand.
The trials and all the pitfalls,
That try to crowd out my joy.
They would hinder my progress,
By their subtle and sneaky ploy.

Guide me and lead me and heal me, oh Lord,
When I can't see the way.
Guide me and lead me and heal me, oh Lord,
And remind to run quickly to stay.
Close to Your side that I might hear,
Your heartbeat steady and true.
It reminds me and comforts me,
Even on those days when I'm blue.

Guide me and lead me and heal me, oh Lord,
Let your glory shine brightly within.
Guide me and lead me and heal me, oh Lord,
And save me from all of my sin.
It is all your work, oh precious Lord,
I take none of the fame.
For if I would garner it to myself,
It would bring only shame.

Guide me and lead me and heal me, oh Lord,
Until the day when I am done.
Guide me and lead me and heal me, oh Lord,
When I will see the Son.
For on that wonderful, glorious day,
My face will surely shine.
As I behold Him in glory,
And all my trials are left behind!

Guide me and lead me and heal me, oh Lord,
With this my next step.
Guide me and lead me and heal me, oh Lord,
To know You in the depth,
Of each decision and fork in the road.
They will be for my good and gain,
When I will listen and follow,
You will make my course and way plain!

Guide me and lead me and heal me, oh Lord,
To that wonderful rugged tree.
Guide me and lead me and heal me, oh Lord,
Where Jesus bled just for me.
His blood has won the victory,
Glory, the sin stain won't remain.
You've covered me completely,
And I'm no longer the same!

# 77

# Glory to God Almighty

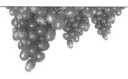

Glory to the Lord God Almighty,
Glory to the precious Son.
Glory to the Spirit so gentle and holy,
Glory to my God, three in one.

You have helped me through each day,
You have guided and lighted my way.
You have counseled me with Your love,
And covered me with wisdom from above.

Glory to the Lord God Almighty,
Glory to the precious Son.
Glory to the Spirit, so gentle and holy,
Glory to my God, three in one.

You hold my hand firmly in Your grasp,
When I am lost and cannot find the path.
You bring Your light to my darkest hour,
And remind me with You I never need
    cower.

Glory to the Lord God Almighty,
Glory to the precious Son.
Glory to the Spirit, so gentle and holy,
Glory to my God, three in one.

You hold tightly onto those I love,
You shelter, shield, and guide from above.
You call them to run quickly to hide,
Into Your love with You to forever abide.

Glory to the Lord God Almighty,
Glory to the precious Son.
Glory to the Spirit, so gentle and holy,
Glory to my God, three in one.

Your counsel is ever sweet,
It swiftly and surely guides my feet.
You sift my heart and affections too,
Until I become more and more like You!

Glory to the Lord God Almighty,
Glory to the precious Son.
Glory to the Spirit, so gentle and holy,
Glory to my God, three in one.

# 78

# A Slice of Eternity

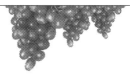

And He was saying to them all, "If anyone wishes to come after Me, he must deny himself, and take up his cross daily and follow Me. For whoever wishes to save his life will lose it, but whoever loses his life for My sake, he is the one who will save it. For what is a man profited if he gains the whole world, and loses or forfeits himself? For whoever is ashamed of Me and My words, the Son of Man will be ashamed of him when He comes in His glory, and the glory of the Father and of the holy angels. (Luke 9:23–26)

I looked when He broke the sixth seal, and there was a great earthquake; and the sun became black as sackcloth made of hair, and the whole moon became like blood; and the stars of the sky fell to earth, as a fig tree casts its unripe figs when shaken by a great wind. (Rev. 6:12–13)

"Let us rejoice and be glad and give the glory to Him, for the marriage of the Lamb has come and His bride has made herself ready." It was given to her to clothe herself in fine linen, bright and clean; for the fine linen is the righteous acts of the saints. (Rev. 19:7–8)

Then I saw a new heaven and a new earth; for the first heaven and the first earth passed away, and there is no longer any sea. (Rev. 21:1)

Do we ever stop to consider all that is at stake as we interface with others throughout our daily routine? That man honking his car horn when you do not accelerate quickly enough at the change of a light, the woman who speaks crossly to her whining child in the store, the teenager who knows so much more than his parents, the unreasonable supervisor whose expectations could not even be met by Superman—each of these people is precious in the sight of God. They are not merely physical bodies that move through our days. They are each a small slice of eternity resident within an earthly body. They each have an eternal destination, one that will shock and surprise many when they find their "good" efforts were not sufficient to earn them a reservation in heaven.

A slice of eternity walks among us. It is your pesky neighbor, your gossipy coworker, your annoying relative, your persistently whining child, your loving spouse, your dearest friend, and even your worst enemy. Each is a slice of eternity walking around on this material earth. The physical landscape that spreads before us and assails our senses every moment is only here for the blink of any eye. Everything we vainly chase after and labor long and hard to possess will one day fade away into nothingness as the creation is consumed with the fire of God's cleansing. This earth will be no more, the sun and moon will cease to shine. Even the stars will fall from the sky. All that remains is God, His heavenly host, His created people, God's Word, and the evil one and his band of demons. All else will be utterly consumed, and the evil hordes do not stand a chance in front of a holy and just God!

As the mists of our daily, ordinary tasks swirl about our feet, the perspective of the eternal softly fades into the background. We become consumed with solving the next problem, earning the paycheck, and meeting the next bill. Physical needs must be met, and we rise to the challenge because their call is so persistent and so immediate. We are intentional to work in a way to accomplish our goals and satisfy our earthbound dreams. The pursuit of these aspirations often drowns out the still, quiet voice that would lead our hearts to hunger for something far bigger and grander. God offers to share the wonders of His heart of love with us. Will we listen? Do we even dare to reflect on the magnitude of all that our God has planned for us? We have the opportunity to join with the vision of heaven to reach the hurting and meet the unspoken cry of desperation of mankind. Whose eternity will our witness impact?

Those who we rub shoulders with do not intersect with our lives by accident. They are there by divine design. Our God knows the special gifts He has deposited within us, and He sees how those gifts can be uniquely used to touch and inspire all those we meet. It may be a smile, a kind word, an act of mercy, or a heartfelt prayer of supplication that would meet the need of the moment. We cannot see into the heart of another, but the Spirit can. We need to listen intently to His gentle nudges and doggedly follow through when He moves on our hearts. Our witness may only be one more nugget the recipient tucks away in his or her memory bank. Yet one sweet day the Lord will have deposited enough seeds and brought enough nourishing water into their souls to cause those seeds to sprout into salvation. Imagine the Lord saying, "Well done, good and faithful servant, enter into the joy of your Master" as He reviews how each thought, deed, word, and prayer worked together to further increase the scope of His kingdom. (See Matt. 25:21.) How much eternal impact are we creating?

God convicts our hearts ever so gently. So then what are we to do? Do we hold loosely the things of this earth, or do they captivate us and garner the majority of our attention? Honestly look at all those around you. Could it be that God has caused your paths to cross so that you can show them the way to an eternity of peace, glory, and incredible joy? Could you be the one who shows them how to alter their eternal destination? Will you risk and reach out to care and love? Will those pieces of eternity next to you rejoice in the courts of your God because you took the risk and loved in the name of Jesus? May God give us each the grace to see with His eyes and consider the truth that each person we see is a slice of eternity walking among us. Eternal man is still breathing. Their destination can still be altered. Rescue is still possible. Let's risk all to win some!

# 79

# The Proclamation

## Our Present-Day Practice of Communion

> For as often as you eat this bread and drink the cup, you proclaim the Lord's death until He comes. (1 Cor. 11:26)

When we take communion, to whom do we proclaim the Lord's death? When we pronounce the message of the gospel, the target audience is often those who have yet to bow the knee to Christ. Yet as we take communion in our churches, the unsaved are usually in a minority in our midst. Praise God, whoever is in our midst during communion will come under the message of the shed blood and broken body of Jesus. The sacraments speak very clearly to all of us in regard to the beautiful sacrifice of Christ on our behalf. This act of reverence and obedience speaks both to the redeemed and natural man. We do not know the spiritual condition of those who fellowship with us. It is not ours to judge. The full message of the gospel is held within the elements, and God cautions us to handle the bread and wine with great awe and reverence. Woe to us if we do not explain the significance of this event to all and caution those not yet covered by the blood of Christ to abstain. God knows our hearts, and He urges us to not take communion in an unworthy manner. (See 1 Cor. 11:27–34)

A closer look at this passage reveals that within communion, our proclamation is also to God Himself. It says, "I believe, I rejoice, and I accept and remember once again the terrible price Christ paid for my sin." It says, "It was *my* sin that bound Him to the cross, *my* sin that pierced His side, *my* sin that whipped Him and pushed that horrific crown of thorns onto His precious head. *My* sin mocked Him and spit at Him, and *my* sin denied Him. *My* sin continued to bear the weight of responsibility for all of this until God opened my eyes and brought me to sweet salvation through the blood of the Lamb." We proclaim all of these things in our spirits unto God when we receive communion. And God is pleased.

Our proclamation is primarily first to God, then to the other believers and nonbelievers with whom we share this moment, but it does not stop there. It is a dynamic, powerful, shake-the-earth proclamation to all the angels and principalities that continually surround us, both angels of light and darkness. Imagine the enemies of the cross cowering as we take the cup, shaking as we drink the wine. They are like caged animals snarling, but for that moment they are unable to attack or maim because the sweet, precious blood of Jesus is flowing over and through His people once again. This is why it is so crucial to take the cup in a worthy manner. When we do not, we are in reality mocking the horrible price Christ paid to win us back to God. In effect we are joining with the forces of evil as they continue to malign God's people in a vain effort to negate the power of the cross and mock God.

Take stock. Do you revile God by your indifference, by your unwillingness to confess besetting sin, by your refusal to let go of pain that surrounds your soul and threatens to drown your spirit? When you prepare to take the cup, beseech the Lord to examine your spirit and reveal all that is displeasing to Him and therefore in reality a blockade to righteousness in your spirit. Then listen—closely, carefully listen. Confess all God reveals, and worship the only one who is able to cleanse you from all unrighteousness. As you bow in your spirit yet again before the wondrous cross, the jeering voices of our enemy's battalion are for a moment silenced as they see the powerful blood of Jesus covering His people, and they shudder.

# 80

# Hearken to the Heartbeat of God

"Therefore let all Israel be assured of this: God has made this Jesus, whom you crucified, both Lord and Messiah." When the people heard this, they were cut to the heart and said to Peter and the other apostles, "Brothers, what shall we do?" Peter replied, "Repent and be baptized, every one of you, in the name of Jesus Christ for the forgiveness of your sins. And you will receive the gift of the Holy Spirit. The promise is for you and your children and for all who are far off—for all whom the Lord our God will call." With many other words he warned them; and he pleaded with them, "Save yourselves from this corrupt generation." Those who accepted his message were baptized, and about three thousand were added to their number that day. (Acts 2:36–41)

And the rich man is to glory in his humiliation, Because like flowering grass he will pass away. For the sun rises with a scorching wind and withers the grass; and its flower falls off and the beauty of its appearance is destroyed; so too the rich man in the midst of his pursuits will fade away. Blessed is a man who perseveres under trial; for once he has been approved, he will receive the crown of life which the Lord has promised to those who love Him. (James 1:10–12)

I have a message from God in my heart concerning the sinfulness of the wicked: There is no fear of God before their eyes. (Ps. 36:1)

The time is short. Many voices swirl about us in an attempt to lead us astray. If we will listen carefully, we can hear the voice of the Lord crying out in the wilderness, "Come to me all you who are weary and heavy laden and I will give you rest … for my yoke is easy and my burden is light" (Matt. 11:28, 30).

Which will you choose—the ease and apparent delight of the world or the solitary, lonesome walk of pursuing God will all of your heart, soul, and mind? It takes no resistance to be drawn away to pursue our own passions and pleasures. God has no delight in those who will not bend or turn their ear to His voice that has been crying out over the generations.

He still calls, "Come, come, My children, for in Me there is rest, comfort, hope, and peace. In the world you will have trouble, but take courage, I have overcome the world. Do not wonder about the fiery ordeal that threatens to overcome you. I see it, I know it, and it will not overtake you if you will turn to Me. It is your choice. Will you feast on today's pleasures and reap sorrow for the opportunities missed? Opportunities that, out of My grace, I provided for you before the foundation of the world so you might walk in those good works and come to know Me more? Will you join with those who have chosen the narrow road and honor Me above all else?

"You cannot have both the exaltation of men and the presence of God. If you continue to seek after My kingdom and the ways of holiness, there will come a point in time when you will be called to choose ease and satisfaction or holiness, righteousness, and the glory of the King. Where is your allegiance divided? I am that I am. There is no other. Why do you think you can find your satisfaction in anything but Me? There is no other. Where have you traded your allegiance? Where did you lose that first love? Repent of your selfish ways, turn from your own pursuit, and honor Me with all that you have, not just with your lips. I abhor deceit, and doublespeak has no place in the lives of My children.

"Turn to Me, My child. Seek first the kingdom of God. Be done with lesser things. I am the Alpha and Omega. I hold your life in My hands. How could it be that I would not give you all things that you need to accomplish My will for you? Will you listen, will you turn, will you trust, and will you follow?"

Holy fear is a good and precious thing. How dare we become buddy-buddy with God almighty! We must exalt Him, for He alone is worthy. We must honor Him in word, thought, and deed, for He alone sees into the heart of man and knows his ways before they occur. We must walk and not grow weary. Though the days become darker and hearts are increasingly hardened toward the goodness of God, we cannot give up. We must continue to proclaim His excellence, His mercy, and His grace.

We must join with Paul, saying, "I have become all things to all men, so that I may by all means save some" (1 Cor. 9:22). Who is God calling you to walk alongside, that they might catch a deeper glimpse of Jesus in you?

> Your lovingkindness, O LORD, extends to the heavens, Your faithfulness reaches to the skies. Your righteousness is like the mountains of God; Your judgments are like a great deep. O LORD, You preserve man and beast. How priceless is Your lovingkindness, O God! And the children of men take refuge in the shadow of Your wings. They drink their fill of the abundance of Your house; and You give them to drink of the river of Your delights. For with You is the fountain of life; in Your light we see light. O continue Your lovingkindness to those who know You, and Your righteousness to the upright in heart. (Ps. 36:5–10)

# 81

# Earth's Pain, Heaven's Gain

Be strong and courageous, do not be afraid or tremble at them, for the LORD your God is the one who goes with you. He will not fail you or forsake you. (Deut. 31:6)

For whatever is born of God overcomes the world; and this is the victory that has overcome the world—our faith. (1 John 5:4)

Trust—a simple word but one of the world's most complex concepts to appropriate and live out. Trust calls us to lean into what we cannot see, feel, touch, or experience. It challenges us to completely abandon our safety net and walk out on the tight rope, knowing full well we may fall at any second. Honestly, left to our own devices, we will most certainly fall and plunge headlong into ruin, despair, deceit, and hopelessness—but for God. He calls us to follow Him without knowing the path, only the end result—heaven. If we were to truly grasp and understand the glories of heaven, this road would look less burdensome and the hardships would truly become joy—because of God. He uses everything to equip and fit us for His eternal call upon our souls.

Yet for a while, we are called to trudge on. God's sweet voice urges us to fly when our feet are covered with mud and anchored to this earth. He calls, "Rise up, child, and enter into your destiny. Be done with lesser things. I know what you need. Look at the lilies of the field. They are clothed in all their glory. How will I not care even more for you, My child?"

We look at the externals and yearn for more. God so desires to give us the more, but it is the more of the kingdom and its righteousness, goodness, mercy, and peace. We have been given all of these things at salvation. What are we doing with them? God sees the heart, and it is a meek and honest heart that delights Him, not one caught up in all the trappings and externals of this world. The heart that seeks His glory and His reputation and yearns to hear His voice is one that brings a smile to God's heart.

So, are you bringing joy to heaven with your heart attitude? Are you filled with praise and adoration? Or are you mired in worry, care, and concern for those you love and care about? It is the heart that is anchored in praise in spite of the hardships—the one that can look above the muck of this world and reach up to heaven with a song of the redeemed—that will soar in spite of any temptation or trial. These hearts that can look to heaven for their fulfillment will then have the ability to refocus here on earth and bring the encouragement and counsel that this hurting world needs so desperately. They will not be words of platitude, which sound grand leaving the tongue but fall empty, hollow, and fruitless upon the recipient's spirit.

The heart's cry birthed in pain and sorrow that feebly reaches toward the Father will be met in a way that is so full, so complete, and so right that heaven's balm will flow down to bind up, heal, and minister. It is then, out of the healing of woundedness, that the greatest help and ministry flow. Those who have been forgiven much love much because they have truly tasted and seen that the Lord is good. So let us take our empty, broken vessels unto the Lord and patiently wait while He fills them with the bounty of heaven's oil and then faithfully go forth to pour out what God has poured in. We will be forever changed, and corporately the body will be moved closer to loving Jesus with all of their hearts, souls, and minds. We will reap all of this because we chose to allow God to break us, remold us, and shape us for the sake of His sheep, not for our own benefit. Are you willing?

> For this reason I say to you, do not be worried about your life, as to what you will eat or what you will drink; nor for your body, as to what you will put on. Is not life more than food, and the body more than clothing? Look at the birds of the air, that they do not sow, nor reap nor gather into barns, and yet your heavenly Father feeds them. Are you not worth much more than they? And who of you by being worried can add a single hour to his life? And why are you worried about

clothing? Observe how the lilies of the field grow; they do not toil nor do they spin, yet I say to you that not even Solomon in all his glory clothed himself like one of these. But if God so clothes the grass of the field, which is alive today and tomorrow is thrown into the furnace, will He not much more clothe you? You of little faith! Do not worry then, saying, "What will we eat?" or "What will we drink?" or "What will we wear for clothing?" For the Gentiles eagerly seek all these things; for your heavenly Father knows that you need all these things. But seek first His kingdom and His righteousness, and all these things will be added to you. So do not worry about tomorrow; for tomorrow will care for itself. Each day has enough trouble of its own. (Matt. 6:25–34)

# 82

# A Godly Secret

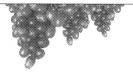

Is it not to divide your bread with the hungry and bring the homeless poor into the house; when you see the naked, to cover him; and not to hide yourself from your own flesh? Then your light will break out like the dawn, and your recovery will speedily spring forth; and your righteousness will go before you; the glory of the LORD will be your rear guard. Then you will call, and the LORD will answer; you will cry, and He will say, "Here I am." If you remove the yoke from your midst, the pointing of the finger and speaking wickedness, and if you give yourself to the hungry and satisfy the desire of the afflicted, then your light will rise in darkness and your gloom will become like midday. And the LORD will continually guide you, and satisfy your desire in scorched places, and give strength to your bones; and you will be like a watered garden, and like a spring of water whose waters do not fail. Those from among you will rebuild the ancient ruins; you will raise up the age-old foundations; and you will be called the repairer of the breach, the restorer of the streets in which to dwell. If because of the Sabbath, you turn your foot from doing your own pleasure on My holy day, and call the Sabbath a delight, the holy day of the LORD honorable, and honor it, desisting from your own ways, from seeking your own pleasure and speaking your own word, Then you will take delight in the LORD, and I will make you ride on the heights of the earth; and I will feed you with the heritage of Jacob your father, for the mouth of the LORD has spoken. (Isa. 58:7–14)

God's economy is so simple. It all deals in the currency of faith—a faith in Christ alone. It is alive and fresh and therefore produces works of righteous and holiness. What does God require of us? Only that we love Him more than our very lives! But as we lay down our lives, He gives us so much more. He calls us to bend down, turn around, and open our ears to the cries of those who are downtrodden and hopeless. We hold the treasures of heaven in our hearts. We must give them out freely, just as we have so freely been given the glories of new life in Christ. God is calling us to be His hands, His feet, and His voice in the midst of a wicked and perverse generation. Are we really listening, or have we become too comfortable?

As the saying goes, you can never out-give God! So what hinders the full joyous expression of our pouring out an offering to Him that is heavy laden with a spirit of joyous thanksgiving for all He has done? Is it because we have been blinded and placed our security in the wrong things? Look at what God promises us if we will do life His way, extending a hand to the poor and drawing together to honor Him on the Sabbath. He promises us a delight in Him that will cause us to ride on the heights of the earth!

True Spirit-led praise surmounts any obstacle and reorients the way we think, perceive, and process the events around us. Corporate worship that focuses on God's glory fuels a spirit of praise and adoration. It is one of those precious moments when iron sharpens iron. If we fully yield ourselves in praise, honor, and adoration when we gather corporately, God fills our spirits with His glory. This births an attitude of reverence that will beckon to us throughout the week to draw aside to worship and honor Him. If we will take away a piece of the burning Holy Spirit fire of worship that is unveiled in our times of corporate worship, it will fuel our spirits each time we draw aside to honor and obey God. This is one reason why God tells us not to forsake our assembling together! In these times of corporate worship, He fuels a passion in our hearts that will burn and draw us ever closer to His heart. Our only natural response is to give away all that He has poured into us, and we begin to shine with the glory of God! As this glory impacts our everyday world, our hearts will turn from our personal pleasures as we begin to listen to the cry of the truly needy, both in spirit and in the flesh. All that we own is at God's disposal, for it is all His to begin with. As we hold out open hands with a loving heart, this world will indeed be changed as it sees the love of Christ pouring forth from His people.

As we deliberately turn from pursing our own plans and align our attitudes with our Father's heart's cry, He pours out His blessings upon us. They are so abundant that we truly begin to see and understand that our cup really does overflow with the presence and provision of God. If we will honestly give to those in need, not out of a sense of charity or obligation but from a wellspring of the Father's love, God will give back so much more. He promises us that we will shine with light like that of the dawn, and our righteousness will go before us and His glory will be our rear guard. What more could we want? If God's righteousness goes before us, He will open doors of opportunity that we weren't even aware existed! As we walk through those doors in obedience, God's glory will be our rear guard. That means wherever we walk and whatever we accomplish, the aftertaste will be one of God's glory. Those we give ourselves for will not see us but will behold the glory of God! Wow!

Indeed, as we begin to grasp and hunger for this type of outpouring, we will certainly become less and Jesus more. Isn't that really the cry of all our hearts? As we continue to lean hard into God and give as He directs, He promises to hear and answer when we call, to guide us and satisfy us in those scorched places when we cannot clearly see His presence. Indeed we will come full circle again and realize that Jesus is truly all we need. After having run hard after Him and given when and how He directs, our agreement with God's ways is no longer just a mental assent but a true life's experience. Jesus met us in all our ways, and we will have seen a manifestation of His glory. We will have experienced the abundance of His provision in ways so deep and profound that it will take more than eternity to praise and thank Him for all He has done!

# 83

## None Like You

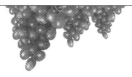

You are righteous and good and
    pure and holy,
Oh Lord, there's none like You.
You are stronger than the
    strongman,
You're good and holy.
Oh Lord, there's no one like You.

Your mercies pour forth to Your
    children,
Your counsel's incredibly sweet.
Oh Lord, Your glory we see now,
As we humbly sit at Your feet.

You are righteous and good and
    pure and holy,
Oh Lord, there's none like You.
You are stronger than the
    strongman,
You're good and holy.
Oh Lord, there's no one like You.

Why would I run to another,
When You hold all that I need?
The sway of sin becomes faint now,
As Your glory covers my dreams.

You are righteous and good and
    pure and holy,
Oh Lord, there's none like You.
You are stronger than the
    strongman,
You're good and holy.
Oh Lord, there's no one like You.

My Lord, my Savior, Redeemer,
You are my closest friend.
You're dearer than a brother,
In You there is no end!

You are righteous and good and
    pure and holy,
Oh Lord, there's none like You.,
You are stronger than the
    strongman,
You're good and holy.
Oh Lord, there's no one like You.

# 84

## Empowering Presence of His Love

Arise, oh sleeper,
Awaken the dawn,
The keeper of your soul,
Awaits.

To converse with you,
And comfort you,
To offer His love,
And enjoy its return.

He is ever watchful,
To protect and guide,
You are never alone,
Or away from His side.

Yet I know that I,
Still have so far to go,
So teach me and lead me,
Dear Lord of my soul.

Strengthen me, Father,
To face the new day,
For dawn has broken,
And stolen away.

The sweet dreams of slumber,
Visions of a love so pure,
Its presence still lingers,
And makes my steps sure.

For to live in that love,
Is life's greatest call,
To bend low and hear,
The cries of the small.

To offer to them,
The same peace that I've found,
While tarrying with my Savior,
On His ground, which is sound.

His love will not falter,
Be shaken, or moved,
For His Word is steadfast,
And it has been proved.

Through centuries of faithful,
Followers of Christ,
They loved Him and followed,
Throughout the trials of life.

Their teachings and counsel,
Still stand today,
And though many refute them,
They won't go away.

God's Word stands forever,
It is pure, undefiled,
It brings hope to the helpless,
And worth to the child.

The simple find comfort,
But the proud reject,
Its inherent wisdom,
That would guide every step.

So which will you choose,
To follow this day,
The counsel of man,
Which leads quickly astray?

Or the heart of a Father,
With a love so pure,
His counsel is flawless,
It is safe and secure.

I do try to follow,
To walk hand in hand,
With my dear Savior,
Who has taught me to stand.

Upon His Word, a treasure,
It's sure to delight,
All those who will seek it,
With all their soul and might.

So come follow me,
Walk close by my side,
And I will gladly show you,
Where I've chosen to hide.

I have turned toward Jesus,
With all my trials and strife,
And He leads me onward,
Through this tumultuous life.

He teaches me forgiveness,
Which cleanses the soul,
Of a poison so bitter,
It strives to control.

My mind and emotions,
Which go quickly astray,
When I will not give Jesus,
My troubles each day.

If I hoard them, ignore them,
They only fester and grow,
Stronger and bigger,
To torture my soul.

They shout hopeless and helpless,
Are you to defend,
Your worth and your being,
So where is your Friend?

So lead me and teach me,
Dear Lord on this day,
There is nothing so wretched,
That You can't wash away.

Memories so deep,
And the sting of their sin,
Their remorse and the shame,
Which would draw me within.

To wither and stumble,
And rot from within,
But Jesus says humble,
Is where to begin.

As soon as I offer the sin unto Him,
Its power's destroyed,
Its piercing is vanquished,
His blood's employed.

To cleanse me and heal me,
To make me all new,
I will stand in glory,
So how about you?

My Lord is my Savior,
My joy and My Friend,
He is closer than a brother,
His love is like none other.

So come to me, Jesus,
I offer today,
My thoughts and my life,
My future will stay.

With You forever,
I no longer fear,
The onslaught of evil,
Cannot my life steer.

I am bound up with Jesus,
He's my law and my love,
I will ever seek Him,
And His counsel above.

So lead me on, dear Savior,
Be my strength and my guide,
Teach me and heal me,
In You will I hide.

'Til one day I shout glory,
This life is all done,
I am finally home,
And I see the Son!

# 85

# The Cornerstone

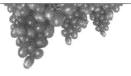

> Therefore thus says the Lord God, "Behold I am laying in Zion
> a stone, a tested stone, a costly cornerstone for the foundation,
> firmly placed. He who believes in it will not be disturbed."
> (Isa. 28:16)

Jesus; is there any sweeter name on earth? He is the center, the glue, the foundation, and the One who holds all of history together. Jesus. Almighty, Powerful. Wonderful. God! He is of inestimable value. His worth cannot be measured or ascertained. He was tried and tested by His travails on this earth. The perfect one was tested and came forth shining as burnished gold. Why would perfection need to be tested? Testing indicates a need for learning and improvement, but perfection by its definition cannot be improved upon. Could this period of earthly training all be done so the finite could catch a glimpse of the infinite? Could it be so we who have ears to hear would have our hearts softened to the point that we would be willing to believe that He truly is the chief cornerstone?

In Him all things hold together. He is indeed the perfect and righteous cornerstone that fits together, aligns, and holds in place His universal church. Anything that is not built on Him will not stand and will not endure. It will be washed away like that proverbial house built on the sand. Jesus; He is the beginning and the end. He was there before the world began; He spoke it into being! And He will be there to welcome His children home when we draw our last breath. In between these two momentous events, He promises to never leave or forsake us as we walk through these years on earth. Oh, what a wonderful Savior!

Our Lord's words are succinct, yet as one turns to them again and again, they hold multiple layers of truth and wisdom. Truly man can never out-think or reason greater than God! Yet how often we try to bargain our way and plead our case and limited understanding before the throne of grace. Our God is so loving and kind. He will never turn aside the true-seeking heart. His patience with us is as boundless as the heavens and as deep as the seas. We see into that mirror so dimly, and our understanding is at best skewed with selfishness and our personal viewpoint. How He longs for the day when the mists will be cleared and we will see Him face to face. God fully knows us now. There are no twists in human thinking or activity that can surprise Him. Yet even in the fullness of His understanding, He longs for the day when we shall fully behold Him and become as He is! God longs for us—what a thought!

We in our flesh hunger to know Him more fully. We groan with the weight of our limited understanding of God as we run this race for the imperishable prize. Yet as we labor and continue to strive for a deeper love and understanding of our Lord, He reminds us of one simple truth. It is a truth plain enough for the simple to grasp and profound enough to keep the astute wondering at the mystery of it all. It is all summed up in one word, one name: Jesus. There is nothing God does that is not done through His Son or without the movement of the Spirit. They cannot be separated, however much man tries!

Our God builds everything upon the shed blood of Jesus. He is indeed the true cornerstone. He is the only firm foundation that will stand throughout the ages and endure all the struggles and wars of man. He alone is worthy to hold everything together. Indeed, He holds all of the history of man in His hands. The wonder of it all is enough to engage our attention for all eternity. As God describes this incredible cornerstone, if we listen closely, we can catch a glimpse of the Father's the heart and passion for His creation. God has firmly placed this wondrous, tested, costly cornerstone in place, and it will not be moved.

He could spend all of Scripture extolling the magnificence of the Son, yet in one breath the Father switches His attention from the glory of His Son to the state of fallen humanity. How He longs for us to be in fellowship with Him! He calls us to heed and believe in the cornerstone, for it is in Him that we can have a faith that will not be disturbed or dismayed. Hear Him calling, "In the world you will have trouble, but take courage I have overcome the world!" (See John 16:33.) God paid the ultimate price:

the sacrifice of His Son. This victory cost Him the agony of the cross, all for one reason: to win back His children with a love that is secure and complete. We must continue to return to the shadow of the cross and ever cling to its healing power. All else will disappoint and eventually leave us bereft and yearning for truth.

# 86

# Leaving a Legacy

Sojourn in this land and I will be with you and bless you, for to you and to your descendants I will give all these lands, and I will establish the oath which I swore to your father Abraham. I will multiply your descendants as the stars of heaven, and will give your descendants these lands; and by your descendants all the nations of the earth shall be blessed; because Abraham obeyed Me and kept My charge, My commandments, My statues and My laws. So Isaac lived in Gerar. When the men of the place asked about his wife, he said, "She is my sister," for he was afraid to say, "my wife," thinking, "the men of the place might kill me on account of Rebekah, for she is beautiful." (Gen. 26:3–7)

Blessings inherited, mistakes repeated. In Isaac we see the promises made to Abraham being passed down to the next generation. He did not receive these promises based on his attitudes or behavior but solely on the merit of how his father walked with the Lord. God is always faithful. God promised, and God delivered. God chose to bless Abraham, and as a child of that blessing, the promises were passed down to Isaac.

What path are we providing for those walking behind us? Our life with God has the potential to extend blessings upon our children that will far outlive our years on earth. With each decision, we can run either toward God or away from Him. The grace and peace God pours out over us as we obey Him are more than enough incentive to follow our Lord. Yet our God is much bigger than our imagination. His grace and goodness toward His children are so beyond abundant that we would be totally overcome if we were able to glimpse even a portion of His favor toward us. He covers us, comforts us, and blesses as we struggle to obey Him. He remembers every act of faithfulness that we have long forgotten and weaves them together to create a tapestry of grace that He can then lay over the shoulders of our children. We tend to walk mired in the perception of today, which is good, because God tells us that each day has enough trouble of its own and not to borrow tomorrow's trouble for today. Yet our children will have the perspective of seeing how our choices and faithfulness impacted us, and they will experience either a trail of blessings because of us or walk under a travail of sorrows that can only be broken by the blood of the Lamb.

God calls us to be faithful in the little things, in the minutiae of life. As we obey and reverence Him in the small things, we build up a life of faithfulness with each brick, stone, and piece of mortar that constructs our life's journey. Our history with God strengthens us for the next pothole because we have previously tasted of His goodness and faithfulness. But the fruitfulness of a faithful life goes so much deeper. It has the potential to rain down a legacy of blessings upon our children that will follow them throughout their lives. They will be able to stand on our spiritual shoulders and glean even more of our God, in part because of our faithful walk. So what is the legacy you are leaving for those you love?

Even though God will honor our faithfulness and bless our children because of it, these blessings do not make them immune to sin. Isaac, even as a child of the promise, still fell into the same sin his father did by professing his wife to be his sister. Self-preservation raised its head again. This speaks to the responsibility each one has to walk in obedience and faithfulness to the Lord. The enemy prowls about like a roaring lion, seeking who he can devour. (See 1 Peter 5:8.) We are often most vulnerable when the patterns of behavior we grew up with percolate in our souls and whisper temptations of fear or lust. If we act on those perceptions and lean on those learned attitudes, we will find we are quickly walking in the same mistakes our parents made. The same will be true of the ones following us. What is the legacy we are leaving, faithfulness or folly?

This reflection is a good attitude check. It helps to remove our eyes off ourselves and grants us a bit more of a godly perspective. Yet if we linger here too long, we can fall into one of two traps. The first will be that of pride, patting ourselves on the back because of the good we have done. Very subtly our focus will shift from honoring God to rejoicing in the good we have done—good works that He in His love created for us to do! This is so ludicrous from God's perspective that it is almost funny.

The other pitfall is to embrace a concern and worry for all the water that has already passed under the bridge. Memories of lapses of faithfulness and selfish living can hamstring us with terror as we realize the full potential they can have to impact and shape our children's character. This is why Paul tells us to keep pressing on toward the upward call of Jesus, for if we don't the past will immobilize us. (See Phil. 3:12.) Those sins that have been forgiven by Jesus' blood have no claim on us. Don't go grabbing them back to ruminate over them. Leave them under the blood! God's grace is sufficient for today; walk in the newness of today.

Rejoice, for as you follow your Lord, you are bringing joy to His heart. He takes the beauty of your life's choices that honored Him and molds them into a lasting legacy that will bless and inspire many generations to come. So keep on following Jesus. Persevere, and know that as you obey, not only are you storing up those heavenly treasures, but you are blessing those watching in ways only heaven will reveal at the end of the age. Keep on following, dear one. God will be pleased, and your children will indeed rise up and call you blessed!

# 87

# Depth of Trust

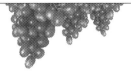

Blessed is the man who trusts in the LORD and whose trust is the LORD. For he will be like a tree planted by the water, that extends its roots by a stream and will not fear when the heat comes; but its leaves will be green, and it will not be anxious in a year of drought nor cease to yield fruit. The heart is more deceitful than all else and is desperately sick; who can understand it? I, the LORD, search the heart, I test the mind, even to give to each man according to his ways, according to the results of his deeds. (Jer. 17:7–10)

Heaven's treasures are completely contrary to the pull of natural man's desires. God calls us to dwell with Him and walk with a heart filled with hope, faith, love, and trust. We have these treasures of the heart available to us all because He has met us with a love that cannot be quenched. He calls us to a child's simple faith that will trust Him regardless of the evidence that tempts us to question and doubt His goodness. To trust is to throw all of our eggs in one basket because there is no backup plan. This can only be done when the object of our trust is firm, sure, unassailable, and totally available. Trust, to bear fruit, must have as its object something or someone who is faithful, true, and immovable. It does not shift with the sands of time. It weathers the storm and survives unaltered. It shines with a rightness and goodness that generations of man cannot quench or snuff out. Given these parameters, the only one worth trusting is God almighty Himself. We are only as secure as the one in whom we trust. Are we building our lives on His faithfulness and steadfastness, or are we aligning ourselves with the shifting shadows that look so solid right now but will vanish quickly like the morning mists when the Son rises?

Any student of Scripture will gladly testify to the righteousness and trustworthiness of God. He wrote the book, and we are merely a comma within its vast text. Yet in the minuteness of this common, simple man lies the vastness of hope of eternity. Its treasures, abundance, and fullness are opened by a God-ordained key—the key of trust. We trust in Jesus' sacrifice for our salvation. So too we must trust in Him for every grand plan and simple detail that covers our lives. Yet, as we ponder this facet of trust, it appears that there is much more to its implementation than what is simply discerned. God says that we are blessed when we trust in Him and when He is the object of our trust. At first glance it appears that these are one and the same, but are they really? When one is trusting *in the Lord*, it implies that he is looking up to God to help, deliver, and direct him in a particular situation or circumstance. He is looking to God for the need for the moment, in the daily details of life. He is seeking God as counselor, comforter, guide, and friend. The perception of His trustworthiness is linked to how we view His intervention and involvement in the moment of our experience.

However, when our trust *is the Lord,* our focus is completely on Him, His nature, His love, and His saving grace won on the cross. We become awe-bound as we gaze upon Him. One glimpse and we are totally immersed in the grandeur and glory of His presence. When *the Lord is our* trust, we are leaning into Him for who He is—almighty God—not because of what He can do for us. It is the spirit that cries with glad abandonment, "You are God and I am not, and all that truly matters is Your glory!"

The journey must begin with this—anchoring the soul on the cross and the awesome and intense victory won through the cruel sacrifice of God's Son. It looks to God as Savior, Rock, and Redeemer. It cries out, "I have no hope for heaven but for You." All work, all effort, and all self-focus fall away as we gaze upon the one whom we have pierced. It is in this moment, when we give absolutely everything we have, everything we are, and everything we dream to God, that we have begun this process of making Him our trust. This is the foundation upon which everything else is constructed. We must be anchored by the Rock. Once our feet are secured to God our Rock through the precious blood of Christ, we can begin the journey of *trusting in Him* for every moment of every day. Yes, to know the fullness of God and to taste His pleasure and blessings, we indeed must trust the Lord and trust in the Lord. Thus begins a continual journey of discovered delights as we lean into the only one who can be trusted for all eternity.

# 88

# Unwavering Holiness versus Sterile Christianity

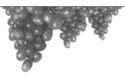

Jesus said to them, "Did you never read in the Scriptures, 'THE STONE WHICH THE BUILDERS REJECTED, THIS BECAME THE CHIEF CORNER STONE; THIS CAME ABOUT FROM THE LORD, AND IT IS MARVELOUS IN OUR EYES'? Therefore I say to you, the kingdom of God will be taken away from you and given to a people, producing the fruit of it. And he who falls on this stone will be broken to pieces; but on whomever it falls, it will scatter him like dust." (Matt. 21:42–45)

Catch a glimpse of the radical purity and aggressive possessiveness of God's love, and your perspective will be changed forever. There is no other. None other will love us, endure with us, stretch us, purify us, challenge us, grow us and then encourage us in the midst of the battle when all looks bleak and hopeless. We are called to be holy as He is holy. As holiness rubs up against a sin-filled world, there will be sparks, raging fires, and conflict. Are there holy sparks in your life? Where is the passion of God burning like an unrelenting fire in your spirit? Has your routine become so comfortable, so predictable that not even a tidal wave could move you from your well-dug trench of predictability? This is sterile Christianity, and it is a place where we all strive to dwell.

How we love security! Could it be we have placed our security in the wrong things? Our Lord had no place to lay His head as He walked on this earth. How is it that we spend so much time and money to enrich and bring comfort and pleasure to ourselves and yet turn a deaf ear to others?

Where is the love of God in His people? The world will know us by our love for one another. We have moderate success here, but this is not the end but only the beginning as we walk in the revealed love of Jesus Christ. We must let it flow through us to touch everyone and everything we rub against in the pursuit of this life.

God's holiness burns with a passion and fierceness that nothing can quench. It is pure, constant, and unwavering. It will tolerate no sin, and it hates that which is lukewarm. There is no place for sterile Christianity in God's economy. God yearns for His people to hunger and thirst for what honors and pleases Him—to spread His holy glory throughout all the earth. There is no greater passion or call, yet all too often we get so consumed by the dailies of life that we ignore the passion of God's heart. We miss the God-ordained moments He spreads throughout our days to honor Him and to testify to the beauty and wonder of His love. How we need a radical makeover of the passions of our hearts!

Jesus promises that as we fall upon Him for mercy, we will be crushed— not shattered, just crushed. He will put us in His mortar, grind us with His holy pestle, and lovingly begin a process of purification that will continue until the day we see Him face to face. If we resist this process, the pressure of refinement will increase with a persistence that will not let up until we begin to beg for mercy and turn once again to the maker of our souls. When we willingly yield to His fiery love, the process of sanctification stings and reminds us that the work of purification is not yet done. As we walk on in this journey with a hunger for God's holiness, we find that as He reveals more and more of the sin that stains our hearts, we first weep with Him over these things. Then when freed from them, we can even laugh at how powerful they looked and how hopeless we felt until the glory of God pierced sin's hold on us. With one breath from heaven, we are set free! Nothing can stand against a move of God's hand!

In the process of this journey, we must continually ask God to search our hearts. Slowly and steadily, He will remove our selfish desires and give us the passions of His heart. There could be no better trade. If we are willing, He will free us from sterile Christianity and cause us to burn with the fire and passion of His heart of holiness. Let's run to Him while there is time and ask for this type of makeover that will last for eternity!

# 89

# Grace

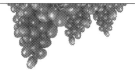

> Turn to Me and be saved, all the ends of the earth; for I am God, and there is no other. I have sworn by Myself, the word has gone forth from My mouth in righteousness and will not turn back, that to Me every knee will bow, every tongue will swear allegiance. They will say of Me, "Only in the LORD are righteousness and strength." Men will come to Him, and all who were angry at Him will be put to shame. (Isa. 45:22–24)

Have you ever stopped to consider the grace of God, to honestly ponder it? It is so deep and rich and thick and wide. It is a grace big enough to cover the whole earth. God's grace runs deeper than any ocean; it is more intimate than our closest thought and more intense than any finely tuned laser beam. It is so complete that it invades every subatomic particle in our being. He even dwells in all the intricate areas of space, that which is in between bone and marrow and soul and spirit. His grace enters into the fray between warring parties. His grace is instantly available in the midst of any fight or argument, if we will only reach for it. His grace is everywhere and is available to everyone. It flies to the highest height and descends to the lowest depth.

It covers not only our actions but also every intention yet to be acted upon. It encourages us when our actions or attitudes are not quite good enough and also when we fail to act upon God's promptings. It hovers over our memories to heal and deliver us. It flies in front of us to guide us through every moment we have yet to experience. It is a shelter for those who go behind us, whose years will vastly outnumber our own earth-bound days. It cannot be exhausted; it cannot be bought or earned. God's grace is free and accessible any moment of any day. It even covers us in our unconsciousness and shelters us in our dreams! Hallelujah for grace! It guides the wandering sinner home. It restores the weary and comforts the brokenhearted. It gives unreservedly even when we don't understand it or even desire it. It shelters us from the full consequence of our actions and loves us even when we spit in God's face. It is freely given through the blood of Jesus to all who will follow Him and trust in Him for their deliverance. It forgives every action and thought that falls short of God's glory. I am so thankful that we live in the season of grace.

Yet there will come a day when the era of God's grace, which we largely take for granted, will end. There will come a day when there is no more time to draw near to God for forgiveness with repentant hearts. There will be a time when heaven turns a deaf ear to those seeking for the life preserver of Jesus' blood as they see the end of this age. It will be too late—too late when the trumpet sounds. Jesus will descend in the twinkling of an eye, and then it will be too late. He will come back for his own. Are you giving Him your full allegiance today? Are you ready?

> For of His fullness we have all received, and grace upon grace. For the Law was given through Moses, grace and truth were realized through Jesus Christ. No man had seen God at any time, the only begotten God, who is in the bosom of the Father, He has explained Him. (John 1:16–18)

> Let it be known to all of you and to all the people of Israel, that by the name of Jesus Christ the Nazarene, whom you crucified, whom God raised from the dead—by this *name* this man stands here before you in good health. He is the STONE WHICH WAS REJECTED by you, THE BUILDERS, but WHICH BECAME THE CHIEF CORNER stone. And there is salvation in no one else; for there is no other name under heaven that has been given among men by which we must be saved. (Acts 4:10–13)

# 90

# Shelter Me

A song of hope and dependency upon God

Come let us go up to the mountain of the Lord, to the house of the God of Jacob. He will teach us His ways, so that we may walk in His paths. (Isa. 2:3)

Shelter and lead me and teach me, oh Lord,
And lead me all of my days.
Shelter and lead me and teach me, oh Lord,
That I would follow Your ways.
Oh Lord, You're higher than my thoughts,
Your ways are pure and clean.
So shelter, lead, and teach me, Lord,
That I would say what I mean.

Shelter and lead me and teach me, oh Lord,
I have no hope but for You.
Shelter and lead me and teach me, oh Lord,
For You alone are true.
This world, it turns to darkness,
As fast as it can run.
I would be totally helpless,
If not for the gift of Your Son.

Shelter and lead me and teach me, oh Lord,
I want to come back to You.
Shelter and lead me and teach me, oh Lord,
Make my heart ever true.

My thoughts can be so restless,
You see and know my ways.
Your love, it will teach and counsel me,
And cover me all of my days.

Shelter and lead me and teach me, oh Lord,
To bring You all of my praise.
Shelter and lead me and teach me, oh Lord,
To look for You in these days.
For You alone are worthy,
You're high and lifted up.
Yet You bend down low to see me,
And lovingly fill my cup.


Shelter and lead me and teach me, oh Lord,
To love You with all that I have.
Shelter and lead me and teach me, oh Lord,
To honor You in the good and bad.
I cannot add You on, dear Lord,
After my plans have been laid.
For You know the end from the start,
And will impart Your plans to my heart.

So shelter and lead me and teach me, oh Lord,
To honor You all of my days.
Shelter and lead me and teach me, oh Lord,
To seek You with my praise,
To gladly offer You praise,
To always bring You my praise.

> Stop regarding man, whose breath of life is in his nostrils; for
> why should he be esteemed? (Isa. 2:22)

# 91

# Forever My Lord

Holy, holy, righteous, and true
Hallelujah, Hallelu
Holy, oh holy, oh righteous is He
Glory to the Lamb of God

*So Lord, come to me, guide and lead me on*
*Open my eyes, my heart to gaze upon*
*The glory of Jesus so faithful and true*
*My Savior, He's forever my Lord*

He is merciful, gracious, long-suffering
He's King, Savior, and Lord
Faithful to His children, the ones that He loves
Oh my Lord, why won't I truly worship You?

*So Lord, come to me, guide and lead me on*
*Open my eyes, my heart to gaze upon*
*The glory of Jesus so faithful and true*
*My Savior, He's forever my Lord*

All glory and honor belong to Your name
My Lord, You are ever and always the same
Those who have gone before now reside by Your side
They see Jesus completely, there's nothing to hide

*So Lord, come to me, guide and lead me on*
*Open my eyes, my heart to gaze upon*
*The glory of Jesus so faithful and true*
*My Savior, He's forever my Lord*

So Lord, let me walk on toward Jesus this day
Let His glory surround me and light up my way
For I falter and fall when I don't heed the call
Please quicken my spirit to give You my all

*So Lord, come to me, guide and lead me on*
*Open my eyes, my heart to gaze upon*
*The glory of Jesus so faithful and true*
*My Savior, He's forever my Lord*

My wisdom is faulty, my vision is weak
I can't see the end, but today do I seek
To hear Your sweet voice and Your counsel today
Oh dear Lord, come quickly and with me please stay

*So Lord, come to me, guide and lead me on*
*Open my eyes, my heart to gaze upon*
*The glory of Jesus so faithful and true*
*My Savior, He's forever my Lord*

Oh Jesus, You're sweet, You're so wonderful
There is none other who compares to You
Yet I rush headlong toward the call of the day,
When, dear Lord, You are beckoning, stay

*So Lord, come to me, guide and lead me on*
*Open my eyes, my heart to gaze upon*
*The glory of Jesus so faithful and true*
*My Savior, He's forever my Lord*

You call me to linger and seek Your face
Amazing to enjoy the warmth of Your embrace
Yet I miss it because I won't stop to seek
The wonder and beauty of God loving the meek

*So Lord, come to me, guide and lead me on*
*Open my eyes, my heart to gaze upon*
*The glory of Jesus so faithful and true*
*He's my Savior, He's forever my Lord*

*He's my Savior, He's forever my Lord*

*Forever my Lord*

Revive me according to Your lovingkindness, so that I may keep the testimony of Your mouth. (Ps. 119:88)

If these devotions have encouraged you consider sharing them with those you love. "Throwing Grapes and Moving Mountains" can be found at the following sites:

- www.westbowpress.com

- www.barnesandnoble.com/book

- www.amazon.com/book